# ALLIED PRISONERS OF WAR IN CHINA

YANG JING

ACA PUBLISHING LTD

Published by
ACA Publishing Ltd
East Wing
Holmbush House
Crawley Road
West Sussex
RH12 4SE
+44(0)20 3289 3885
info@alaincharlesasia.com
www.alaincharlesasia.com

Beijing Office
+86(0)10 8472 1250

Author: Yang Jing
Translated by ACA Publishing Ltd
Editor: Matthew Keeler
Cover art: Daniel Li

Published by ACA Publishing Ltd in association with the People's Publishing
House

The greatest care has been taken to ensure accuracy but the publisher can accept no
responsibility for errors or omissions, or for any liability occasioned by relying on its
content.

Paperback ISBN: 978-1-910760-29-1
eBook ISBN: 978-1-910760-58-1

A catalogue record for *Allied Prisoners of War in China* is available from the National
Bibliographic Service of the British Library.

# CONTENTS

These brutal reprisals upon helpless victims evidence the shallow advance from savagery, which the Japanese people have made … We serve notice upon the Japanese military and political leaders as well as the Japanese people, that the future of Japan as a nation, in fact the Japanese race itself, depends entirely and irrevocably upon their capacity to progress beyond their aboriginal barbaric instincts.

    – General George C Marshall

Humility must always be the portion of any man who receives acclaim earned in the blood of his followers and the sacrifices of his friends.

    — President Dwight D Eisenhower

The whole history of the world is summed up in the fact that, when nations are strong, they are not always just, and when they wish to be just, they are no longer strong.

    – Sir Winston Churchill

# INTRODUCTION

In the Pacific theatre of the second world war, both the scale of the conflict and the nature of the battlefields were unprecedented. The numbers of those captured by the Japanese forces, including Allied army prisoners of war, exceeded anything known in the past and went beyond all expectations.

Mistreatment of prisoners of war, contravening international conventions, became one of the major war crimes of the era. The notorious cases of the Bataan Death March and the Burma-Thailand Railway of Death, in which so many prisoners were maltreated and so many perished, joined the Nanjing Massacre as the three biggest wartime brutalities addressed by the post-war International Military Tribunal for the Far East.

Looking at the history of warfare – either in China or other countries – it is undeniable that prisoners of war are a product of all wars. The Pacific war could not have been an exception. But the terrible brutality and the forced labour experienced by Allied prisoners of war can truly be said to be without precedent. By way of illustration, the Japanese took 270,000 Americans prisoner during the war; of these, 110,000 died in captivity. In the three months beginning 8 December 1941, 22,000 Australian troops fell prisoner, and by the end of the war only 13,400 survived; the death rate was more than one in three.

The prisoners who left the battlefield did not leave the war itself. On the contrary, they became a new kind of resource for the Japanese military. They either became a labour resource on which the Japanese could depend for the further operation of the war machine or a resource to be used in a last-ditch military struggle. In this war with no historical precedent, Allied prisoners of war were an ever-present and significant element from beginning to end. The war they experienced, the hardships they suffered and the sacrifices they made were decisive factors in the ultimate victory in the Pacific war.

This book is about the POW camp in Mukden (now known as Shenyang), established by the Japanese military to lock up those taken from the battlefield in Southeast Asia and use them as forced labourers. The special features of the camp – the high mortality rate and the presence of high-level skills and highly-ranked officers among the incarcerated population – starkly illustrate the historical conditions that the Japanese military created in their POW camps, as well as their supreme aim of turning the POWs into labour resources in service to their war machine. This book offers testimony to the terrible circumstances and bitter experiences of the POWs, and it relates how the Japanese military tried to use captured senior officers as instruments for the preparation of a last-ditch defence, in violation of international norms and humanitarian agreements. It provides a basis for today's generation to form their consciousness and make their own evaluations. It helps us to penetrate more deeply and offers a unique perspective on the Pacific war. The historical legacy of the lives and sufferings of these Allied POWs provides not only ironclad proof of the Japanese military's war crimes but also a warning for the future – that history never be forgotten, that peace be treasured and that opposition to war be deeply instilled.

Looking back at these events, the hardships, struggles and sacrifices of the Allied POWs not only prove the crimes of the Japanese military; they also bear witness to the anger that the Chinese military and the Chinese people shared with the Allied military and nationals in the context of the worldwide struggle against fascism. Above all, what should not be forgotten is that the Chinese army and the Chinese people shared common burdens and a common destiny with the Allied armies and peoples, fighting together against the common enemy and defending their common interests.

We can also see that the Allies maintained their unity and their common spirit both in the way they liberated the POWs at war's end and in the way they handled the defeated Japanese forces. This spirit of cooperation was a vital guarantee for the establishment of the post-war international order.

Today, looking broadly at the global situation at war's end, we cannot but be deeply affected. To choose to 'forget' history, or to make conscious choices 'to no positions' would not only be contrary to the protection of the post-war order; it would also send a mistaken signal to 'rightist forces'.

The vicious treatment that the Japanese military meted out to Allied POWs is cause for profound contemplation about the meaning of civilisation itself. So-called 'civilisation' has already become little more than a tool, a material device. Civilisation must be based on human nature. The logic of the powerful rising to the top does violence to human values and serves only to promote the homogenisation – the unipolarity – of man's thinking.

Thus, more than 70 years on, we proceed on the principle of 'not forgetting the past, with the past as the guide for the future'.

We cast our eyes over the ways in which the values evident in history can enlighten today's minds. Let us part history's misty curtains and tell the true story of what happened in the Mukden POW camp, in order to refresh the minds of our contemporaries.

# TO LIVE OR TO DIE

ON 7 DECEMBER 1941, the Japanese Imperial Navy attacked Pearl
Harbor, the principal US naval base in the Pacific, crippling the US
Pacific Fleet. On 8 December, Japanese forces struck south into
Southeast Asia, sending forces to attack Hong Kong, Singapore, the
Philippines, the Dutch East Indies (today's Indonesia) and Burma.
With the declaration of war on Japan by the US, the UK and China,
now Allied, the Pacific war exploded in full fury. The European and
Asian theatres of war mingled together, and what had been regional
conflicts became world war.

The origins of the Pacific war lay in deep-seated conflicts
between Japan on the one hand and the US and the UK on the other.
In 1938, the Sino-Japanese war reached a stage of relative
stalemate. Because of its massive losses along extended lines of
battle over long periods of time, Japan's financial, material and
military human resources were proving severely inadequate.
Meanwhile, Japan's efforts to project power and secure strategic
resources in areas controlled by the US and the UK were becoming
more and more superficial. In July 1941, the US and the UK froze
all Japanese assets and cut off all oil shipments to Japan, reducing

Japanese oil imports by 80%. They also cut off major portions of Japan's supplies of wheat, cotton, zinc, iron ore, bauxite and manganese – all critical for military use. The US and the UK laid down the following conditions for the elimination of these sanctions: Japanese forces were to leave Indochina (today's Vietnam, Laos and Cambodia) and China. Would Japan abandon its aggressive ambitions?

Japan's final answer was conflict with the US, the UK and other Allied nations.

Japan's strategy in the Pacific theatre was to use Malaya and the Philippines as bases from which to conquer the Dutch East Indies from both sides, first seizing the outer islands and oil fields and destroying Allied military forces, and then combining their forces for the assault on Java, expelling American, British and Dutch power and establishing complete control over the area's rubber, oil and non-ferrous metals resources.

The campaign went even more smoothly than supreme Japanese headquarters had imagined. Among their goals, the conquest of the Philippines aimed to eliminate any threat from the US. If they could drive out the Americans and then seize Guam and Wake Island, Japan's forces would be able to construct a defensible zone. On 10 December 1941, the Japanese opened a massive assault on the Philippines. The Americans quickly lost the initiative, and Manila soon fell. The US forces withdrew to the Bataan peninsula.

On 12 March 1942, General Douglas MacArthur, commander of US forces in the Far East, withdrew from the Philippines to Australia, where he issued his famous pledge to the people of the Philippines: "I shall return." On 22 March, Lieutenant General Jonathan Matthew Wainwright was the Allied commander in the Philippines. On 3 April, the military situation deteriorated severely, as the Japanese launched a massive attack against the entire US-Philippine defence lines with 100 aircraft and 300 heavy artillery pieces. On 9 April, the US commander on the Bataan peninsula,

Army Major General Edward King, realising that his forces could no longer resist, announced their surrender, and the Bataan peninsula fell to the Japanese.

This was the biggest surrender in the history of both the American and Philippine armed forces. More than 60,000 Filipinos and 10,000 Americans were taken prisoner. The prisoners went on a forced march, northwards from Mariveles, at the southern tip of the Bataan peninsula, to San Fernando, and from there to the former Philippine army training centre at Camp O'Donnell, (subsequently turned by the Japanese into a POW holding camp). On that forced march of 100km, 15,000 prisoners of war died from hunger, thirst and exhaustion, or were beaten to death or shot by Japanese soldiers. This was the infamous Bataan Death March, burned into the history of warfare. The vast majority of the prisoners held at the Mukden POW camp had taken part in that march, so our story begins there …

2
_____

# THE DEATH MARCH

OLIVER C ALLEN, who became POW #362 at the Mukden camp, had arrived in the Philippines just weeks before the attack on Pearl Harbor. He joined the 19th Bomber Squadron, based at Clark Field, the largest US base in the Philippines. On 8 December, ten hours after the assault on Pearl Harbor, the Japanese launched a massive attack on Clark Field, destroying all the planes on the ground there.

Allen recalled: "At Clark, all our planes got destroyed on the first day. We had nineteen bomb planes down on a southern island, Island Mindanao. They survived, but they didn't help us much. They sent one or two planes into Clark, but then they flew away, and we never saw them again. And then we just became isolated."

Christmas came two weeks later. Each American at the base was allotted half of a can of beans for Christmas dinner. On 2 January 1942, American forces were holding the Bataan peninsula. Allen and his comrades packed their gear and advanced towards Bataan. That night, when the troops reached Bataan, they distributed their rifles to the other soldiers who had only a tiny amount of training. Allen remembered it this way: "I'd been a country kid, so I knew a little bit about how to fire rifles, but some of the boys didn't. We took one change of socks and a change of underclothes, and they said we wouldn't be there long. But we stayed till the war ended. That was from New Year's Day till April ninth."

On that day, Japanese forces began a two-pronged attack on the Bataan peninsula. The defending forces put up stiff resistance. Allen recalled: "Our unit had been up on the front, and we were forced back to organise our reserve line. And there, for the first time, I met the commander, General King, who commanded Bataan. He had been given orders to fight to the last blood. King got his little white flag, and he met the Japanese and surrendered the peninsula. He saved many lives."

Allen became a prisoner at 4pm on 9 April. Some of the younger members of his ten-man unit still wanted to find a way to break out of the Japanese encirclement, but when the order to surrender came, the whole unit was captured. "We had some hand grenades on our belts, but we never had a chance to use them," Allen recalled. All of Allen's weapons were thrown into a dump.

The Japanese marched their prisoners to a short airstrip, perhaps once used by old-style P-40 fighters. After lining up their prisoners, the captors ordered them to sit cross-legged on the ground. "I think they were moving their artillery right in behind us," said Allen. "We were just a short distance from the island of Corregidor, and the object was our artillery. They would use us as a muffler, or they could fire over us so our artillery on Corregidor would not fire back. But under the side of my leg, along the coverall, there was a little zipper pocket. And I had a hand grenade down there, and it bothered me. We lined up, and they made us sit down and cross our legs. I happened to be at the end of the line. I thought it must be a rock or something down there. I pulled the hand grenade out in my hand. The guard was standing directly behind me, looking right at me."

Allen handed the grenade over to a Japanese soldier. The soldier ran with the grenade over to a watchtower ten metres away, but at that very moment, an artillery shell, fired from the defenders on Corregidor, exploded. In the confusion that followed, four prisoners managed to flee, escaping the disaster. Allen, in one breath, raced away for about two miles.

Allen recounted: "We lay on the side of that road late that night. The next morning, we were woken and pushed back on the road, and they lined us up. And that was the beginning of what they called the Death March."

At the outset, the prisoners were marshalled into four companies, spread out far from one another, so that the entire marching line was very long. Japanese guards marched in the spaces separating the four contingents of prisoners, frequently replacing one another. "We started along the road at just after eight in the morning on April tenth," said Allen. "Some Japanese soldiers passed us marching in the opposite direction. We had not gone a mile when the Japanese troops surged among us, searching us one by one." The Japanese soldiers seized the prisoners' food and emptied their water canteens. They smashed the prisoners' food bowls with the butts of their guns and handed the shards back to them. They plundered the prisoners' helmets, destroyed them and then threw them by the roadside.

Allen recalled that each of them had a small Bible, signed by the president as gifts to the entire unit. He carried his Bible on his body. One of the Japanese soldiers found it and made a prayer gesture with his hands before returning it to Allen. Thanks to that good luck, Allen was able to hold on to a family photo that he had kept inside the Bible. When they were searched, many of the POWs had Japanese-made souvenirs or other items. For that, they lost their lives, because the Japanese troops thought that such items must have been seized from the bodies of other Japanese.

Allen recalled an incident on the third day of the march: "I ran into two of my buddies from my airfield. One couldn't make it. So I moved in, and we let him swing on our shoulders, and helped him along. My buddy who was still strong had sugar and crackers. His name was Ray Thompson. I said to him: 'Ray, let's have some of that cracker and sugar.' Ray said: 'We save this for when times are rough.' I said: 'I don't see any rougher time than right now.'" The three men collapsed on the road. The soldiers behind them trod over Allen's shoulder. They could only rise to their feet and stagger onwards.

Before they had gone two miles, the Japanese carried out a 'sun treatment' against the POWs. Just as the sun's brilliance was at its most brutal, the POWs were herded into a wire cage to fry. There was no protection. When they were first driven into the enclosure, the men had to strip off their possessions and throw them into a pile. Allen said that he held on to his Bible, but his backpack and sugar had to go.

The POWs waited, dry and hot, for a whole day inside the sun treatment cage. When they set out on the road again, the Japanese demanded that no one help anyone else. Everyone had to make his own way, and lifting up another soldier was especially forbidden. A soldier stricken with malaria could go no further. "He finally died by the side of the road. Before he died, I was beside him, and he would say, 'I'm still all right'. But after a day or two he died. It became just a combination of nightmares," said Allen.

Later on, Allen met another comrade among the marching prisoners. The man was too sick to rise. He told Allen he would be going home. Allen said to him: "Glad to hear that. I know you told me about your dad, your mama back home, and about your little sister." But his comrade simply said: "I can't get back home. I'm afraid for my country. I lost the war. I'm going to heaven." He died two days later. Allen could only try to bury him where he fell. "Of course it was sad, but it had to be done," he said. "We went out in the morning and dug a grave. Just dug a hole in the ground, as far as you can get with the tool. We went out in the afternoon and took all the dead. The Japanese wouldn't let you lay them in – you had to drop them in. Drop them, and cover them up."

Robert D Rosendahl (Mukden POW #127) was serving as an air-force mechanic in Bataan and later joined the land battle. "We lost all our aircrafts and the aerial part of the war," he said. "So they converted us into infantry and put us on a beach patrol to keep the Japanese from coming around the other side."

A detachment of Japanese troops came ashore in the area guarded by Rosendahl's men and withdrew after a brief firefight. Rosendahl himself took a Japanese soldier prisoner. He recalled: "He swam up the beach, but he was wounded in the shoulder, lost lots of blood. He was exhausted." Rosendahl and one of his comrades loaded the wounded Japanese soldier onto a stretcher and brought him to an army truck, which conveyed him to a field hospital.

On 9 April, Rosendahl heard the order to surrender. "Our front line had collapsed. We were out of ammunition, practically. We had food restrictions for three months. Everybody was tired, and we had very little food. We were told to destroy our weapons," he said.

Rosendahl and his team destroyed their weapons and moved to the assembly point for the surrendered American forces. He recalled: "The Japanese lined us all up and marched us up to the hill, out of Mariveles. I remember how harsh the Japanese were. We started this march out of Bataan. A lot of guys had dysentery and malaria and poor health, with bandages, and we shouldn't have been walking. There was very little water. We had no food. During my march of five days, I received one ball of rice. As we marched along, we saw many who had been killed, and many who had been badly abused – especially the Filipino troops. I saw so many dead soldiers along the road. They had been marching ahead of us. Anyone who broke ranks was killed immediately. The Japanese used their swords and their guns to do the killing. This is what happened on the Bataan Death March."

The troops marched by day. When they gathered for the night, there was no sanitation. When Rosendahl reached the designated ending of his march, he was put to work burying corpses. "We buried a thousand bodies," he said.

US Army medical doctor 1st Lieutenant Elmer J Shabart (Mukden POW #4) never forgot his experiences on the Bataan Death March. Along the route of the march, one POW was stricken with appendicitis and in unbearable pain. Shabart had no drugs, no surgical instruments, no sutures. He boiled some water to sterilise, picked up odds and ends of broken glass and thread from the roadside, and performed crude surgery on his comrade. He tore up strips of abandoned clothing to bind the wound. "Do it, doctor," the man cried. "I'm willing to die." There were no orderly medical processes. There were no meaningful sterilisation procedures. Shabart's only goal was to save his buddies.

Once the Japanese forces had taken Bataan, they set about optimising the favourable geographic features of the territory they held as they prepared for their assault on Corregidor, which was defended by a labyrinth of tunnels. On the island, a total of 13,000 American and Filipino troops endured an unbearable bombardment by more than a hundred Japanese heavy artillery pieces. The artillery bombardment was so intense that the Americans thought they were taking heavy machine gun fire rather than field artillery rounds.

The American commander on Corregidor, General Jonathan Wainwright, eventually concluded that further resistance was futile. Military necessity had exhausted his food supplies, adding hunger to the ravages of tropical diseases among his men. Using weapons from the first-world-war era to defend against the Japanese army with its modern arms was little more than an Arabian Nights fantasy. The moment of surrender on Corregidor was only a matter of time.

Three times on 5 May, Wainwright broadcast a ceasefire

proposal to General Homma Masaharu, commander of the Japanese forces, proposing that both sides cease fighting at noon, and pledging that the Americans would raise white flags at Corregidor's most prominent locations while sending representatives forth to discuss surrender terms with the Japanese. At the same time, Wainwright sent a final message to President Roosevelt:

It is with a broken heart and head bowed in sadness, but not in shame, that I report to Your Excellency that today I must arrange terms for the surrender of the fortified islands of Manila Bay. There is a limit of human endurance, and that limit has long since been passed. Without the prospect of relief I feel it is my duty to my country and to my gallant troops to end this useless effusion of blood and human sacrifice. If you agree, Mr. President, please say to the nation that my troops and I have accomplished all that is humanly possible and that we have upheld the best traditions of the United States Army. May God bless and preserve you and guide you and the nation in the effort to ultimate victory. With profound regret and with continued pride in my gallant troops I go to meet the Japanese commander. Goodbye, Mr. President.

At exactly noon on 6 May, General Wainwright ordered the lowering of the American flag and the hoisting of a white flag. This was the bitterest order in his entire military career. A white flag was hoisted at the west entrance to the Malinta tunnels housing US military headquarters, but the Japanese did not respond. The fierce bombardment of Corregidor continued unabated. Wainwright ordered that a surrender message be broadcast again. At about 1pm, General Homma, by the side of Manila Bay, learned that the US forces had already flown the white flag, finally recognising the complete occupation of the Philippines. He ordered his officers to bring Wainwright to meet him, repeatedly demanding that

Wainwright's surrender include all remaining US forces on all defensive lines in the Philippines.

But Homma still did not issue a ceasefire order. He intended to continue to direct maximum pressure against the Americans. The artillery barrage against Corregidor went on, and Japanese land forces continued their assault on the main US garrison in the area around the Malinta tunnels. At that moment, Homma was not only the military victor; he saw himself in a position of strength. He knew he would be in a position to dictate terms in the surrender negotiations that were just around the corner. This psychological superiority reflected the absolute power of the Japanese military on the battlefield.

In fact, both General Wainwright and General Homma were calculating the broader picture as well as the details of the surrender. Wainwright considered the Corregidor surrender as covering only the surrender of his Manila Bay defensive line. He still hoped to maintain the small but viable Visayan-Mindanao Force. These forces, led by General William F Sharp (Mukden POW #1595), had formerly been under Wainwright's command. To protect his overall position, Wainwright had telegraphed Sharp prior to the Manila surrender, transferring his command authority over Sharp's forces back to General MacArthur. But General Homma was unyielding on this point through all the twists and turns of the negotiation with Wainwright. With both sides unyielding, Homma finally stormed out of the negotiation, with the threat that the fighting would continue unless there was a complete US surrender.

Needless to say, by that point, Wainwright had no negotiating power. He had no choice but to order a total surrender. Finally, at 1am on 8 May, by Japanese arrangement, Wainwright broadcast his announcement over Manila's KZRH station: all US forces in the Philippines had surrendered. On 9 May, with the formal surrender in hand, Homma addressed Wainwright: "All forces under your command have surrendered. Your supreme authority is terminated.

You are now a prisoner of war and will be transferred immediately to the Tarlac prisoner of war camp." With that, General Wainwright became the highest-ranking prisoner of war in the history of the American armed forces. The loss of the Philippines, in turn, became the largest-scale surrender in US military history.

When news of the Japanese attack on Pearl Harbor reached the Philippines, Roy M Weaver (Mukden POW #610) was in a hospital, ill with jaundice. He said that when the war broke out, his health took a turn for the better. Weaver was initially a machine gunner, assigned to guard the docks at Cavite, on Luzon Island. Japanese heavy artillery wiped out the docks on 10 December 1941, and Cavite's positions began to shift constantly.

On 28 December, just after they had celebrated Christmas, Weaver was transferred to a defensive position on a little island close to Corregidor, mainly to defend the coast. For the next few months, despite continual bombardment by Japanese planes, Weaver's unit held out until Wainwright's surrender announcement of 6 May. Weaver recalled: "It is impossible to describe my feelings as I watched with my own eyes the lowering of the American flag and the raising of the white flag of surrender."

Val F Gavito (Mukden POW #1026) remembered the tragic lowering of the flag on Corregidor: "I stood on the field and watched the formal lowering of the flag. The mood was utterly sombre. I and a few other soldiers stood on the field. Colonel Bunker issued the order to lower the flag. As the flag slowly came down, we stood at attention, facing the flag. We detached the flag from its lines, making sure it didn't touch the ground. Then we quickly destroyed the flag in a burning pyre we had already lit." After the American flag was completely burned, a white flag was raised. Through all of this, no one spoke. When it was all over, everyone silently returned to his position.

Joseph A Vater (Mukden POW #974) was serving with the 803rd Engineer Battalion, based at Camp O'Donnell close to Clark

Air Base. He recalled: "My squad was made up of artillerymen and marines. After the surrender of Corregidor, as we were making our way to the POW camp at Cabanatuan, the Japanese marched us along the Dewey highway to display us to the people of Manila city." [Dewey was Admiral George Dewey, whose naval forces attacked the Spanish fleet in the Battle of Manila Bay in 1898. The highway was a broad road running along the coastline of Manila Bay, famous for its sunset scenes and its coconut palms.]

From Manila, from Bataan, from Corregidor, most of the 75,000 prisoners from the Philippine battlefields were initially transferred to the three holding camps set up at Cabanatuan, which covered 100 hectares, and were the largest POW sites set up by the Japanese military in the Far East. The site had been the training ground for the 91st Philippine Division; by now it was completely encircled by barbed wire.

By 25 May 1942, the first batch of American prisoners of war from Bataan was placed in Camp 3. Three days later, 6,000 POWs from Corregidor were sent there as well. Another 15,000 American POWs were put in Camp 2. Later, because there was no drinking water there, these Americans were sent to Camp 1. Because many of the prisoners in Camp 1 had come from Bataan and were in bad physical condition, with no medical facilities, a great many men were lost.

"I was the youngest POW from the Bataan Death March," said Robert A Brown (Mukden POW #190), by way of self-introduction. By 1940, the European war was in full swing. Brown's older brother and one of his best friends joined the army. "I begged my mother and father to sign an affidavit saying that I was eighteen when I was really sixteen," said Brown. "I just wanted to get into the army." On 2 October 1940, Brown became a member of the US Army Air Corps, assigned to the 34th Fighter Squadron. In October of the following year, he headed for the Philippines.

Brown recalled: "After Bataan surrendered on April ninth, on the four-day march covering seventy miles, I saw with my own eyes my comrades being shot or cut down. On the march, I saw the Japanese behead two prisoners. They forced us to watch. Horrors like that can't be forgotten. I haven't spoken to very many people about it because they just wouldn't believe me." Even decades later, Brown suffered recurrent nightmares of the Bataan Death March.

After the march, Brown was first put into the Camp O'Donnell POW facility in central Luzon. In June 1942, he was moved again – this time to the Cabanatuan camp. "There, one thousand three hundred POWs died in sixty days. Because I was a medical corpsman, I was put into the most wretched spot, filled with prisoners suffering from dysentery. Everyone there was at the brink of death," he said.

The story of another soldier who had fought on Bataan, Daniel H Roberts (Mukden POW #1483), was equally terrible. In an interview with me in 2012, Roberts said that he was taken prisoner on the eve of Bataan's surrender after he fell ill while carrying out a transportation assignment. The Japanese sent him and three others to a factory near the island of Corregidor. "They lined us up and then beat us with their rifle butts, chains and bamboo rods. The day was overpoweringly hot. The sun blazed directly down on us," he said.

Roberts and the other three men were thrown into a truck, with no idea where they were headed. Finally, they reached the Bilibid prison. Suffering from maltreatment and malaria, twenty to thirty prisoners were dying there each day. The Japanese threw the corpses out to rot in the sun. "When we went on burial detail, we could see what looked like greenish serpents coming out of a corpse's entrails. We had to throw the corpse into the water and then quickly throw some dirt over it," recalled Roberts.

Soon after, the Japanese began to send many of their prisoners to the Japanese home islands or other Japanese-occupied territories as labourers. In June 1942, as they occupied Singapore, Burma and the Dutch East Indies, the order was issued: over the coming year, a railway would be built from Thailand to Burma to secure the materiel needs of the Japanese forces in Burma and maintain their fighting strength, in order to defend against any Allied military attack coming from the Bay of Bengal. That railway would also be vital in serving Japanese military needs for the assault on India itself. The Japanese military required 50,000 POWs and 200,000 forced labourers. With a terrible climate, overworked labourers, food shortages and an utter lack of medical supplies for those suffering from tropical diseases, construction of the railroad cost the lives of 1,600 POWs and more than half of the forced labourers. The Thailand-Burma Railroad earned the name 'Railway of Death'. After the war, the Military Tribunal for the Far East listed the Bataan Death March, the Railway of Death and the Nanjing Massacre as the three biggest Japanese war crimes in Asia.

# 3

# THE HELL SHIPS

"YOU WILL SEE that this is a gorgeous and blooming place, with wonderful foods, fresh seafood and fruit. Nearby, you will find bathing beaches. Truly, you will love Hualian!" Thus spoke a deceitful Japanese officer to General Wainwright as he awaited relocation from the Philippines to Taiwan. After his capture, Wainwright was transferred to six different POW camps: Tarlac in the Philippines; Hualian, Yuli and Muzha in Taiwan; Zhengjiatun (Branch Camp 1 of the Mukden camp); and Xi'an county (Branch Camp 2 of the Mukden camp).

During the Pacific war, the Japanese set up numerous POW camps and assigned a number of ships to the special duty of transporting prisoners. Those ships were crowded beyond imagination. Health conditions were utterly miserable.

Some of those aboard, who had either contracted contagious diseases already or whose bodies were simply weakened, died in transit in the ships. Moreover, in contravention of international custom, the Japanese POW transports did not display the insignia of the Red Cross, with the result that they were frequently attacked by

Allied aircraft, with massive casualties. These POW transport boats were dubbed 'Hell Ships'.

Of the 58 ships that left Manila carrying prisoners of war, six were reportedly sunk by Allied fire, at a cost of several thousand prisoners. Among the dead were 5,000 US POWs. In the end, the Hell Ships carried about 68,000 Allied POWs from Singapore and Manila. Of these, 28,000 perished under attacks by Allied bombardments.

After he gained a new lease of life, William D Miner (Mukden POW #1915) recalled his experiences in one of the Hell Ships. On 13 December 1944, 1,619 American POWs were loaded aboard the Ōryoku Maru. The ship was originally a Japanese mail transport and was pressed into military service when the war broke out. The Japanese troops forced the prisoners into the ship's holds and sealed the hatches. The ship was overpoweringly crowded and stifling. Only half of the captives could even sit down; the rest remained standing. Elsewhere, in staterooms or on the upper decks, rode a number of Japanese military and civilians.

An hour after sailing, the captives below deck were fainting from the heat and the stale air. There was no drinking water. The only water the prisoners had was what they brought aboard with them. But after eight hours, half of the men were at the end of their ropes. By the evening of the first day, the prisoners were like wild men, howling and fighting with one another. Chaos reigned in the blackness of the ship's holds, punctuated only by cries of "Help!". By the morning of the next day, by the thin light of a few rays that shone into the hold, the prisoners could be seen, jammed together at every angle, with fifteen or twenty of them already dead. On the bodies of the dead, especially around their necks and wrists, bite wounds were clearly visible. The men had gone mad from hunger and thirst, and they tried to satisfy their cravings with the blood of their comrades.

On 15 December, something awful happened. The ship had been

under Allied air attack for two days. At about ten in the morning, a bomb exploded within the ship's lower hold where the prisoners were confined. In the space of an hour, the hold was filled with blood and flesh. Two hundred captives were killed. The dazed and panicked prisoners began to surge around the hatches, struggling to get out. The Japanese soldiers standing guard outside the hatches opened fire on the struggling prisoners and even threw hand grenades down into the hold. Even after that, a few captives escaped from the hold and threw themselves into the sea.

The guards continued to fire at the men in the water; even there they could not avoid misfortune. After this calamity, only 1,333 captives remained alive. They were transferred to another ship, Eijiri Maru. But this ship, too, came under Allied air attack, so the POWs were moved again, and they finally reached Japan on 29 January 1945. Of the 1,619 men who set out from the Philippines on the Ōryoku Maru, only 490 stepped ashore.

On 7 October 1942, another Hell Ship, Tottori Maru, set out from Pier 7 in Manila, filled with more than two thousand American POWs, all of them completely in the dark as to where they were going or what the future might hold.

Oliver Allen recalled: "I don't like to think about that journey. Once we were selected, we travelled by train to Manila and went from the train station straight to Pier 7. The ship was a steamer, with two thousand men stuffed in the holds. We could hardly breathe. The ship was bedlam, in complete darkness. As soon as we left Manila Bay, the ship stopped. The prisoners waited in the hold, forbidden to go to higher decks. We had two five-gallon oil cans for toilets, set in two corners. On two wooden pillars in the hold, some boards were nailed up to form a sort of frame. We lived on top of that. So many people crammed so tightly together – we were like sardines. Food was distributed in oil cans strung together on a line. There were no utensils – we ate with our hands. I had part of a little rice box, made of aluminum, and I used it as a sort of food scoop.

Food distribution was chaotic. Some of the men got their hands on a little, while others grabbed a lot. Some men got no food at all. No one managed the situation. No one organised it. It was chaotic and cold-hearted. I will tell you frankly – all basic military discipline was lost. We became men with no feelings because every one of us was struggling to survive."

When James Bollich (Mukden POW #1439) spoke of the horrendous scenes aboard the Tottori Maru, he burst into uncontrollable sobbing: "It was no surprise that men died under those conditions," he said. "At first, only one or two men died each day, and on some days everyone survived. But later, many died each day." Many perished at night, and their bodies were thrown over the side the next morning. But as night came, the despair deepened in the pitch blackness of the hold, as the cries of the suffering crescendoed.

One night, mayhem erupted in the hold, punctuated by howls and the sounds of fighting. In the darkness, no one knew what was happening. The next morning, the prisoners were stunned by what they saw. All along, there had been one prisoner who sat expressionless in a corner. That evening, his mind must have given way. He began flailing wildly with his rice box, smashing at those around him. Finally, the others could stand it no more. They turned on him and beat him to death with his own food box. "Somebody dragged his body out and threw it into the sea with the other corpses. Their suffering and their wild confusion were over. They were free," Bollich concluded.

Robert Rosendahl was also on the Tottori Maru. He remembered: "When October came, we were set up for departure. We went down the rail line to Manila and then were herded onto an old Japanese cargo boat. Two thousand Americans went aboard, and then two thousand Japanese boarded as well. They were headed back to Japan after fighting on the battlefield." It is thought by some that putting the Japanese in the ship carrying POWs was a way of avoiding Allied attacks. Rosendahl was already suffering from dysentery when he boarded the ship, and shortly after boarding he collapsed. Eight hundred POWs were packed in like sardines. "There were no sanitary facilities at all. We just used five-gallon cans lying in a corner, the same kind of cans they used to bring food to us. In the hold, there was no organisation. It was like a zoo. The conditions were just crazy," said Rosendahl.

Three or four days after they left Manila, someone launched a torpedo at Tottori Maru. The ship took evasive action and heeled sharply, throwing all the prisoners around. Near the stern of the ship, all sorts of heavy collisions took place, and several Japanese soldiers were crushed to death. The ship endured two more torpedo attacks but continued on its course, finally reaching Gaoxiong, on the island of Taiwan, before moving on to other destinations.

Though this Hell Ship had been shelled by Allied forces, none of the POWs on board died as a direct result. The filth and overcrowding aboard the ship made for the rapid spread of dysentery and other serious diseases among the prisoners, and some died before the ship reached its destination. As Allen recalled: "Just after we got to Taiwan, fifteen or twenty men were carried away. All of them were either older or very sick and unable to stand. So they were taken off the ship, and we never saw them again."

Once the ship docked at Gaoxiong, the men disembarked, and the Japanese hosed them down with water cannon. Then they were loaded back onto the vessel, which set out again after taking on fuel and drinking water. Rosendahl recalled: "We stopped for four days there. It was extremely hot. The Japanese let us off the ship and washed us down just as though we were hogs. Once we left Taiwan, we arrived at some islands between Taiwan and the mainland. We remained there for a week or so, and then headed for Busan, Korea."

In his diary, James E Brown (Mukden POW #333) wrote:

6 October: Assembled at Pier 7, Manila.

7 October: Boarded the Tottori Maru, a rickety old ship. Loaded in like canned fish. Hard to stand up.

21 October: Two of my mates died. Buried at sea. The Japanese captain snapped in two the American flag we used for the burial service.

27 October: Arrived Gaoxiong. Another man died. Ten men were sent to hospital. Loading of coal land water underway.

3 November: Two more deaths.

6 November: Another one of our comrades died.

7 November: Another death.

Those who died aboard ship were thrown into the water with weights tied to their feet. By the time the ship reached Busan, 29 corpses had been cast into the sea in this way. Daniel Roberts, who survived, noted that the entire voyage to Busan took a month and that some prisoners died along the way: "I remember how they disposed of the corpses from the ship. They would place a body on a long plank at the tail end of the vessel, tip the plank and slide the body straight into the ocean. That was the sum total of the burial for those bodies."

Another POW in the ship was the medical doctor Elmer Shabart, who recalled: "As we continued our voyage, the weather turned colder. The bodies of those who died were taken to the upper deck. We stood silently, while they were thrown into the sea." By that time, a number of the POWs were showing signs of respiratory infections or the beginnings of pneumonia. Shabart could do nothing. "We had no equipment, no drugs," he said. "You could give my life as a POW a title: 'Forgive me. I have nothing with which to treat you.' My helper fell and broke a bone. All I could do was use the lid of a discarded wooden crate used for packing fruit, and a strip of sail cloth, to stabilise the bone."

Rosendahl recalled: "At that time, we were like a herd of beasts of burden, with no idea where we might be headed." When the ship reached Busan, all the POWs were taken off. The Japanese stripped them naked, ordered them off the boat and sprayed them with insecticide. "The purpose was to kill lice. We all choked and struggled for air when they sprayed us," said Rosendahl. Once off the ship, the POWs were gathered together on the pier. The Japanese gave them 'new clothes' – they were actually old Japanese garments, many with patches. "These were items the Japanese had gotten hold of in the 1904 war with the Russians. They kept those clothes all that time and passed them out to us. All of those clothes were forty years old," said Rosendahl. "Then we boarded a train for Manchuria. On the train, we ate the same food that the Japanese were eating. It was the first time we tasted food like this. Until then, all we had eaten was odds and ends. The only water we drank was muddy. Once we landed in Korea, each of us got a cardboard food box with rice and a few slices of fish, topped with kimchi. It was the first time I had eaten clean food."

In Busan, some of the prisoners fell by the wayside. One of them was Bollich. He recalled the day of 8 November 1942, when the ship landed at Busan: "I was sick as a dog. I was weak and had no way of keeping up with the men as they moved on." Bollich and about sixty other POWs were taken off the ship and held, to be sent to hospitals. After several weeks, when their conditions had improved, they continued on their way to Mukden. "As we boarded the train, the Japanese gave us some cans containing the ashes of men who had died at Busan. We carried them with us to Mukden," said Bollich.

In his diary, the medical captain Mark G Herbst (Mukden POW #3) wrote: "On the voyage aboard the Tottori Maru from Manila to Busan, 11 men died at sea. Another 12 were confirmed dead during our stop at Gaoxiong on Taiwan. While we were docked in Busan harbour, another 53 were confirmed dead."

Throughout most of the voyage, General Wainwright had his

own cabin in the ship. Although his life was never in danger, he did not escape from utter humiliation at the hands of his Japanese captors. One day, he was taken on deck and made to pose for a Japanese painter, who intended to produce a picture of Wainwright surrendering to the Japanese. When the painting was done, it was to be sent to the Emperor in Tokyo. Time and again, the prisoners were humiliated for the production of photos or paintings that would be sold for a profit.

When the survivors reached Mukden, their physical condition was terrible. Brown recalled: "By the time I got to Mukden, I weighed 82 pounds. My normal weight was 165 pounds. But my feet were really swollen. I was suffering from beriberi." He hated to dredge up the nightmares he went through on the Hell Ship. "It really was hell," he said.

Silence does not signify forgetting. I visited the Brown home in 2007. It was my fourth visit with Brown. His house was in a mountainous area of northern California, in a little hamlet called Brownsville. Brown told me his ancestors had come to this place in the days when America was opening up the West. After several generations of dangerous, hard work, the Brown family had managed to become reasonably prosperous.

Among the family assets were several hundred hectares of forest land on the outskirts of town. A private family cemetery lies inside this forested property. Brown's parents are buried there. "I deeply hope that I can be buried there, with them, after my own death," Brown told me. But, to protect the natural environment, current regulations require cremation before burial in a private family cemetery. If a person chooses burial without prior cremation, it can only be done in a designated public cemetery. This has caused Brown much heartache. "I really want to lie beside my grandfather, but I am not willing to be cremated. I have already descended into hell, in the Hell Ship and again at Mukden. I have been to hell twice already," he said.

# 4

# THE BELL TOLLS AT MUKDEN

IN THE SIX months after the outbreak of the Pacific war, Japanese forces successfully captured Thailand, Hong Kong, Malaya, the Philippines, the Dutch East Indies, Burma, the Solomon Islands and part of the Aleutian Islands. They captured 27,000 American servicemen and 130,000 prisoners from the UK, Australia, New Zealand and other British Commonwealth members. Dutch prisoners of war numbered about 110,000. Most of the prisoners were incarcerated locally. The Japanese established 104 prison camps, branch camps and transit camps in Mukden, Shanghai, Taiwan, Hong Kong, Hainan, Korea, Malaya, the Philippines, Thailand, Burma and Java.

The prisoners sent to Mukden fell mainly into two categories: those with special technical skills and high-ranking officers. Why these two categories? Because Mukden, the principal city in Manchuria, held special significance for Japan.

Japan saw Manchuria as a lifeline. In the years since the famous Mukden Incident of 1931, the economy of China's northeast had been woven directly into the Japanese war system. A broad and effective industrial system had arisen. Reportedly, by the end of

1944, the Tiexi Industrial District in Mukden included 323 enterprises, accounting for 60% of the value of industrial production for the whole city. By the late months of the war, the value of industrial production in Manchuria actually exceeded the value of industrial production in Japan itself.

As a key industrial city, Mukden drew together the main industries of the Japanese military in northeast China; especially armaments and machinery production. To meet the requirements of advancing the war effort, a huge number of technically competent workers was required. Thus, prisoners of war with technical backgrounds became necessary labour resources for the Japanese forces.

Politically, the 'Manchuria Lifeline' was deeply rooted in Japanese militarist thinking. The military authorities in Japan had put out an order to journalists and public speakers, instructing them to propagate the ideas that "Manchuria is Japan's lifeline" and "Japan must enfold Manchuria". In the days when the news of the Pacific war was all positive, and especially later, when it appeared that the US was going to attack Japan, some voices in Japan advocated abandoning the Japanese islands and concentrating all forces to protect Manchuria. With that in mind, the Japanese military carefully plotted to select certain high-ranking captured officers for transfer to Mukden to use them as bargaining chips when the war was lost.

Against this historical background, the Japanese set about building the only permanent POW camp at Mukden.

The Kwantung Army issued the order to begin construction of the camp on 20 October 1942. By 31 October, the Mukden Temporary POW Camp was set up, under the control of the First Brigade of the Mukden Independent Garrison, taking over grounds of the Northern Big Camp on 1 November. The station commander was Colonel Matsuyama; the general affairs chief was First Lieutenant Terao; the chief surveillance officer was First Lieutenant

Miki Togeru; the intelligence chief was First Lieutenant Murata; Second Lieutenant Yamaura Heisaburō was in charge of provisions; in charge of bedding, utensils, etc, was Second Lieutenant Fukazawa Katsuzō.

On 11 November, the Temporary Camp began taking in prisoners.

There were 1,428 men in the first batch of POWs to arrive at the Mukden camp; 1,328 of them where Americans captured in the Philippines; another 84 were from the British forces (including New Zealanders) captured in Singapore; the remaining 16 POWs were Australian. When the International Committee of the Red Cross visited the camp in 1943, their report noted that the camp held 1,274 prisoners, including 84 from British forces, 16 Australians and 1,174 Americans. Of these, 23 were officers, 545 were non-commissioned officers and 706 were enlisted men. The oldest prisoner was 57, and the youngest was 21. In the following years, the population of the camp changed constantly, as some prisoners were transferred and some died. By 30 June 1945, the camp held 1,709 captives, including 77 newly added Dutch prisoners; 250 prisoners had died, including three shot by Japanese soldiers; one prisoner had disappeared without a trace.

On 11 September 1945, a total of 1,698 Allied prisoners of war were liberated from the POW camp at Mukden.

The Mukden POW camp was advertised by the Japanese military as "the POW camp with the best facilities and the finest management". Japanese military Propaganda Corps visited Mukden frequently, taking pictures, making films and telling the prisoners how their life in the camp managed to be so "comfortable". In reality, however, things were not like this at all. Not only were the prisoners' lives not comfortable, they consisted of compulsory labour, hunger, cold and sickness. In addition, doctors and medicines were scarce, and the Japanese troops treated the prisoners inhumanely. All of this amounted to huge challenges to the POWs' survival.

The American prisoners, for example, had gone through four months of bitter fighting in the Philippines, under terrible conditions and with a desperate shortage of rear support. They were grievously wounded, in body and in spirit. After the surrender, they had endured both the Bataan Death March and the travails of the sea voyage on Hell Ships. Therefore, the health of the American POWs was a mess. Even the commandant of the Mukden POW camp, Matsuda Genji, had to admit as much. He said to visitors from the International Committee of the Red Cross: "At the beginning, when these prisoners came here from the tropics, their physical condition was pathetic. Their clothing and their short trousers were utterly unsuited for the cold of winter in Mukden. A number of them died from respiratory ailments or repeated attacks of malaria."

As a result, in that first winter after their arrival at Mukden, a great many prisoners died. Frigid temperatures and frozen ground meant that bodies could not be buried; they were piled in storage sheds. Rosendahl recalled: "When we got to Mukden, we were shocked by the scene that confronted us. The ground was already frozen when we stepped off the train. It was raining. Everything was coated with ice. The ice on the roads was six inches thick."

The prisoners arrived at an abandoned military camp in the northern outskirts of the city; the locals called it 'Northern Big Camp'. Covering 18 hectares, the camp had formerly been used by the Chinese Army of the Northeast. On the night of 18 September 1931, the Japanese had attacked the Northern Big Camp, seized the city of Mukden, occupied the three northeastern provinces and opened a new chapter in their criminal aggression against China. Now, with the arrival of the Allied prisoners of war, the Northern Big Camp once more played a part on the world stage, drawing tightly together China's battlefield and the global battlefields of the struggle against fascism.

From north to south, the Northern Big Camp was 240 metres long, while from east to west it was 180 metres wide. There was a total of 19 barracks buildings. A hospital, a kitchen, a storehouse, a latrine room and so forth added up to a total of 27 structures. The camp was surrounded by barbed wire a metre and a half high. An inner and an outer course of barbed wire encircled the camp with about two metres between them. This was the "no man's land". No one was permitted to enter that space, and anyone found there would be shot. Steel towers were placed at intervals. Seen from afar, each barracks took on the appearance of a gigantic graveyard.

Rain and sleet fell without end. The prisoners stood in the freezing cold, waiting for the Japanese to arrive. Rosendahl recalled: "We formed two lines and waited a couple of hours for a Japanese officer to come and say something. He dragged the time out on purpose, letting us stand and freeze. At the time, while he was holed up inside, I thought maybe he was trying to let us get cold for a while. Finally, he showed up and made a little speech."

The officer making the speech was the camp commandant, Colonel Matsuyama. He told the prisoners: "Although I am now 57 years old, I am still living under conditions as bad as yours. I have accepted all manner of hardship in order to care for you. We ask you to obey camp regulations rigorously. Carry out all orders and instructions fully. Bow your heads to all Japanese soldiers as a sign of respect."

Rosendahl said: "We couldn't understand a word. He spoke to us in Japanese. Later, there was a translator, but I still basically did not understand, or else I couldn't hear what was being said. After that, we dispersed. Each of us was given a camp number. Mine was 127. We were wet. We were cold. And we were agitated. The Japanese gave each of us a canvas bag. We stuffed our bags with straw to make mattresses. They gave us each a blanket and a Japanese-style pillow – that is to say, a piece of cotton cloth – and a pile of buckwheat shells that we stuffed into the cloth to make a sort of pillow. Then we went to our barracks. The Japanese told us to arrange our individual goods. When the Japanese came in to take roll, they ordered us to answer to our camp numbers. Each person was to shout out his number in Japanese. You had to say it right – if you got it wrong, the Japanese would beat you with their rifles, their swords, or their fists. This was a lesson in quick learning. It was a very tough education."

Oliver Allen remembered: "It doesn't matter what you call it – we breathed a sigh of relief when we got to the Mukden camp. I drew number 362. The first thing we had to do when we reached the camp was sign a 'Promise Not to Escape'. Those POWs who refused to sign were considered to be enemy fighters in a state of war. Everyone was required, at any time and at any place, to write his camp number. We were ordered to learn right away how to say our numbers in Japanese. When we wrote down our camp numbers, we had to shout out our numbers in Japanese in a loud voice, or we would be beaten by the Japanese."

The prisoners soon learned what Commandant Matsuyama meant when he talked about "bad living conditions" in his first address to the new arrivals. They were led into a barracks built partly underground. That was where they would sleep. In the old days, these cells were referred to by the local troops as 'The Cellar'. To keep out the cold, they were built half above ground and half below ground. Rosendahl recounted: "They led us into these rooms that were like trenches. I had no idea what these would be used for. Some people said this was an old training base."

Arthur Christie (Mukden POW #1228) offered this description: "The area the prisoners lived in was about five hundred square metres. There was a stove and six wide plank beds, on which a hundred and thirty-two prisoners slept. Each space was marked with a camp number corresponding to the number tattooed on a prisoner's body."

Although this semi-underground wooden structure did have a

heat-preservation function, in the icy winter of 1942 at Mukden, there was no way to keep the cold from filtering in through the wooden walls. Allen remembered: "That first winter was really very hard. We had been in the tropics before that and had never experienced an icy winter."

Rosendahl added: "It was just too cold. We had no fuel for heat. Heat was available only from December 21st, the first day of winter. Can you imagine? No heat until winter. We finally got a box of about twenty-five or thirty pounds of coal. It was nowhere near enough to warm the entire hall. We had only our own body heat to keep us from freezing in the room. The medic told us to breathe in steam, but where were we supposed to get steam? Every day they gave the prisoners a mess tin of hot water. Even when we were sleeping, we kept that water next to our bodies. This water was supplied once daily. Anyone who drank his water would suffer frostbite."

Rosendahl and many other POWs suffered from typhoid, pneumonia, beriberi and other diseases. "I myself came down with beriberi. My lower extremities swelled badly. If anyone had stuck his hand into my pants, he would not have been able to pull his hand back out. Once the oedema receded, the pain was excruciating; it felt as though my foot had been chopped off," said Rosendahl.

Survivor Russell A Grokett (Mukden POW #319) had clear memories. The temperature at Mukden in November 1942 dropped as low as –40C. When they slept, the prisoners had to use every scrap of clothing they possessed. Even washing one's face required courage. "We put our hands into the water, and when we pulled them out they had turned bright red," said Grokett. He saw with his own eyes some prisoners sit down and never stand again.

British Major Robert Peaty (Mukden POW #24) wrote in his diary:

On our arrival on 11 November 1942, we were put into a

temporary camp, consisting of wooden huts partially sunk into the ground. The framework of upright posts, about 4" x 4", was boarded on both sides, and the space between filled with earth. The roof was of single boards covered with a layer of mud. I would not keep my garden tools in such a shed, but this was actually a Chinese barracks, or hutted camp.

The 'hospital' was no more than one of these huts set aside for the purpose. I was able to secure prints of two snapshots which show these buildings in the background. The 'hospital' had only one bedpan at a time when there were a hundred patients with dysentery, and many died from pneumonia contracted by having to get out from under five or six blankets and go to an outdoor latrine with the temperature as low as sixty degrees of frost.

Though they were now far from the smoky field of battle, the POWs had not escaped from the sense of death around them. Roland K Towery (Mukden POW #858) was one of the many POWs who went through this life-and-death trial. Towery contracted beriberi in the camp because nutrition was so inadequate. He recalled: "The so-called 'clinic' was just another old wooden barracks building. My feet and legs burned as though they were on fire. It felt like nails being driven through them. All I could do was put snow on my legs to try to bring down the pain. Even worse was the terrible swelling. It began in my feet and crept upwards through my legs. When the swelling reached the trunk of men's bodies, they perished."

Towery's condition gradually worsened, and his fever stayed high. Incessant coughing set in, and he grew too weak to stand. Some of the other prisoners brought him to the clinic on a stretcher. Little by little, Towery and the patient next to him became permanent invalids. On his other side, over a period of six weeks, five or six men came and went. A POW would arrive, and after a few days he would die, and another would arrive. The clinic had

31

virtually no medicines; all the sick prisoners could do was 'wait'. To this day, Towery relives the anguished scene in his mind: one of his closest comrades, staggering on bloated legs, crying out, "I can make it, I can make it," before he died.

Major Peaty recorded in his diary for 26 May 1943:

Diagnosis of diarrhoea consists of running the men around the parade ground, (I saw some of them with bare feet). Those who do not mess their pants, or drop from exhaustion, are reckoned to be liars, and told to "go back". A protest has been made, and a change is expected in both methods and personnel.

The bitter cold of Mukden put every life at risk. Every man had to bear the burden of finding enough warmth to stay alive. The POWs hoped that the Japanese would grant them hot food, but the spectre of hunger filled the camp like a haze. Their constant preoccupations were, first, food; second, warmth; third, cigarettes. Food was always the top preoccupation. Starving and freezing in the camp, between life and death, they knew that eating a little more could save a life. Every day, prisoners carried food from the camp kitchen to the barracks in wooden barrels and distributed it to everyone. The prisoners could choose one man as the chow dipper to dole out the food. All the others would stand in line, taking turns to receive their portions.

Towery sometimes served as the food distributor: "Most of the people who did this job didn't do it for very long, because of one conflict or another, but I managed to keep doing it until the end of the war," he said. His secret was simple: before doling out the food, he would put one portion in his own bowl and set it beside the food barrel. Then he would serve everyone else the same portion. If someone was suspicious that he had been cheated, he was welcomed to switch his bowl for Towery's bowl, leaving what he saw as his smaller portion by the food barrel. "That way, no one ever moved to take my own bowl," he said.

Towery considered it an honour to be able to pass out food to these desperately hungry men in this way. Not only did he gain the trust and respect of his fellow prisoners, but it gave all of them an understanding of the real meaning of the Confucian saying, "Do not to do others what you would not have done to yourself." During our interview in May 2007, Towery told me that he had already selected his burial spot in his native Texas, and had written the inscription for his tombstone: "The Chow Dipper."

When the prisoners actually saw the food, they were inevitably disappointed. The first meal at the camp left Rosendahl in despair. He recalled: "Somebody brought in a wooden barrel filled with soup. There was something in the soup – a little corn, some cabbage. The soup was very thin. Everyone got one ladle of it. The doctors told us we would get no more than eight hundred calories a day. That was the way it was through the entire winter, from 1942 into 1943. Many of the men died. The camp stored the corpses. In the spring, as the corpses thawed, wild dogs were drawn to the camp by the stench. We began killing the dogs and eating them. This was the only food we could find outside of our camp rations. I heard that some people from outside the camp wanted to bring food or other things into the camp to make a little money, but it was impossible, and they went away."

To kill the dogs, the prisoners came up with their own dog traps. They placed the traps outside the windows of the barracks, with a bit of bread as bait. Once a dog got inside the trap, they would savagely slam the trap door shut on the dog's neck and drag it inside through the window so they could beat the dog to death. Then they would hang the dog up, just as they might do in a meat market. That was how the prisoners managed to get a little meat, which they hadn't had in such a long time.

Because dog meat was highly calorific, this dog-trapping

'technology' quickly spread throughout the camp, and all wild dogs near the camp became prey. Soon enough, some POWs began selling dog meat inside the camp. The going price was eight ounces of meat for ten cigarettes. But this trade did not last long. For one thing, the wild dogs in the area became fearful of approaching. More importantly, some prisoners found the body of an old Chinese man, devoured by wild dogs, by the roadside.

Because many of the prisoners contracted contagious diseases, all sorts of germs spread rapidly through the camp. The number of sick prisoners reached eight hundred, more than half of all the men there. The camp clinic quickly filled with people suffering all manner of diseases. Grokett came down with viral pneumonia, complete with a high fever that refused to break. But he knew what going to the clinic meant. He held out, determined to fight the disease, but finally one day he felt unbearably cold. He summoned all his energy to call to a Japanese soldier, begging to be placed in the furnace room, and squeezed himself inside the furnace, where the fires had gone out. It was still very warm inside the furnace, and Grokett spent several hours inside. When the soldier reappeared to see whether Grokett was still alive, he discovered that the prisoner was much improved.

The American survivor Robert Brown was a medic at the camp. He had picked up a few simple Japanese phrases and could carry on basic conversations in Japanese. For that reason, he often served for patients lining up or redirecting in the clinic when they arrived to see the doctor. "But I quickly became the top tooth-extracting 'dentist' in the camp. The camp basically had no drugs – dental equipment was completely lacking. Of course, I had had no special training. To take teeth out, I just relied on my hands and my physical strength," he said. Because Brown was strong, and his extractions seemed to cause little pain, many prisoners came to him to have teeth removed.

James Bollich said he had discovered that he was suffering from roundworms. But while the Japanese told him the results of a lab test, no drugs were available to treat the problem, so he remained in limbo. The roundworms gave him stomach cramps much of the time, and finally he decided to try a local remedy he had heard about. Someone had told him that the main component of the oil that collected inside the bowl of a smoking pipe was nicotine. If eaten straight, it could destroy worms. But if the patient ate too much of it, it could be dangerous, even life-threatening. Bollich asked one of the POWs who was a smoker to give him the oil from his pipe. Amazingly, after four or five weeks, his roundworm problem had taken a big turn for the better.

Major Peaty described medical conditions in the camp this way:

Japanese drugs are very strange. Although Japanese medicine is famous, many of those so-called 'gentlemen who pursue the craft' are just one step up from witch doctors. Three American doctors and an Australian doctor told me that powdered rhinoceros horn is commonly found in the Japanese medicinal formulary. I once saw a medicine advertisement: it claimed that the product was effective because it contained powdered pearl. They see cow's milk as a medicine, not a drink, to be dispensed in the same amounts as thistle. On top of that, these doctors told me, when they asked for permission to use opium to treat dysentery, they were authorised to use only one hundredth of the dosage we consider appropriate. The Japanese doctors consider the smallest doses we use as lethal. They have the greatest suspicion of our doctors. What our people might see as a medically necessary amount of opium they tend to see as an amount that could only be for hidden purposes. This reference to opium is only one concrete example – the phenomenon itself was much more widespread. For another example, if we needed to use two aspirin tablets, the Japanese doctors would only let us have a half tablet whose dosage was a twentieth of the dosage we needed. Of course, the

Japanese medics had no prior knowledge of some of the drugs we were using. The way we saw things, the medical equipment there was antiquated and far below necessary standards. For example, we tested everyone for roundworms, and found that 39.6 per cent of us carried them. After conducting detailed and minute investigations, the Japanese announced the results of their roundworm survey, but they said that no drugs were available to use against it, and that they were not sure such drugs could be delivered. On top of that, in the entire camp there was only one dose of an injectable drug used to combat gangrene. The Japanese were fond of saying that in Japan all of these items were plentiful. We found that that was not true. We could see that their troops were wearing uniforms that dated from the Russo-Japanese War of 1905. Just as they were short of clothing, their food and their medicines were in short supply as well. Although we gradually came to hate the Japanese, I have to tell the truth of what I saw with my own eyes.

Thirty-four months went by between the arrival of the first prisoners of war at the Mukden camp in November 1942 and the complete liberation of the camp in September 1945. The acts of atrocity by the Japanese troops throughout those months never ceased. The long period of maltreatment and miserable living conditions contributed to high rates of death among the prisoners.

Statistics relate that the death rate in German POW camps in the European theatre was 1.2%; at Mukden, the rate was 16%, or 250 deaths – 13.3 times the death rate in the German POW camps. Under such inhumane conditions, some prisoners preferred to risk death attempting to escape.

The Japanese military responded to the high death rate at the camp. The commander of the Kwantung Army organised certain members of their Unit 731, Disease Prevention and Water Supply Department into a Temporary Inspection Team and sent them into the Mukden camp to do an investigation of medical conditions. The Kwantung Army headquarters then issued Kwantung Army HQ Order No. A98, which read as follows:

<u>Top Secret. Kwantung Army HQ Order A98 by order of Kwantung Army Commandant, Xinjing</u>

1 February, 1pm

The Kwantung Army Command will immediately and temporarily assign a group of troops under its command to the Mukden POW Camp and orders them to enter the camp under the direct orders of the commandant of the camp. The group shall consist of one medical doctor, four lower-ranking public health workers and officers, and ten health troops.

1. The commandant of the Mukden POW Camp shall, on the basis of the work performed by the assigned group, increase sanitation work within the camp and, as rapidly as possible, restore the full work capacities of the prisoners.

2. The chief of the Water Purification Section of the Disease Prevention Department of the Kwantung Army should send this team quickly to the Mukden POW Camp to assist and guide the centre in its anti-epidemic work.

3. In addition to the regulations established by director of the Military Medicine Department, further and more detailed measures shall be adopted by commanders of the relevant military units.

> — GENERAL UMEZU, COMMANDER IN CHIEF,
> KWANTUNG ARMY

Upon receipt of General Umezu's order, the commander of the Military Medicine Department of the Kwantung Army promptly issued the following instructions:

Instructions from the Head of the Military Medicine Department in Accordance with Order A98 from Army Headquarters

1. The heart of the disease-prevention work at the Mukden POW Camp will be bacteriological examination of the prisoners, starting with examination of the digestive systems of prisoners afflicted with repeated outbreaks of chronic dysentery and amoebic dysentery. Following that, examinations will take place for those suffering from malaria, roundworms and other conditions requiring examination.

2. The required testing equipment will be provided by the Kwantung Army Anti-Epidemic and the Water Supply Department.

— GENERAL KAJITSUKA, COMMANDER,
MILITARY MEDICINE DEPARTMENT,
KWANTUNG ARMY

Major Peaty described in his diary the arrival of the Japanese military inspectors:

13 February 1943: About 10 Japanese medical officers and 20 other ranks arrived today to investigate the cause of the large number of deaths.

14 February 1943: Vaccination for smallpox.

15 February 1943: Two Americans died in hospital; autopsies

being performed on the corpses by the visiting Japanese. Owing to the frozen ground, we have been unable to dig graves for some time, and all the bodies have been kept in rough board coffins in "cold storage".

The Japanese investigators to whom Peaty referred to were part of the team sent by the Anti-Epidemic and Water Supply Department. Details of the investigations at this time appeared in the Highlights of the February Monthly Report on the Mukden POW camp:

Report on the Temporary Disease Prevention Work

21 February 1943

1. Operating Conditions: The Temporary Disease Prevention Unit of the Kwantung Army Disease Prevention and Water Supply Department was organised under Kwantung Army Headquarters Order A98, and on 14 February arrived at the Mukden POW Camp, where it began its work. It completed its investigation of the causes of gastric conditions among patients in the isolation ward on 19 February, with particular emphasis on investigation of dysentery among all patients.

2. Condition of the patients: 247 prisoners suffered from dysentery, out of a total of 1,038 prisoners who evacuated their bowels at least three times between 19 February and today. 124 were admitted to the isolation ward on orders from the military doctors. The other 123 prisoners either described their own symptoms as less severe or seemed healthy. Five prisoners died between 13 February and 19 February.

3. Investigation of the causes of illnesses: The results of the

gastrointestinal examinations of the 124 patients admitted to the isolation ward were as follows:

Bacterial dysentery – 33 testing positive

Amoebic dysentery – 15 testing positive

Green mould mucus – 11 testing positive

Xylococcal mucus – 1 testing positive

4. Observations from autopsies: Nine examinations were conducted. All revealed dysentery. One additionally exhibited Type A paratyphoid.

What merits special attention here is a report by Colonel Nagayama, head of the Treatment Section of the Kwantung Army Disease Prevention and Water Supply Corps, dated 17 February 1943. The report was titled, 'Regarding the Clinical Conditions of Mukden POW Camp Patients Described as Suffering the Ill Effects of Wartime Nutrition'. The report examined the bodies of the POWs and concluded that the American prisoners had suffered from inadequate nutrition in the Philippines before they arrived at Mukden. Then they had endured a month's sea voyage before reaching Mukden amid conditions of bad food and sanitation. Allied attacks on their ships further damaged their health and were detrimental to their nutrition. But the entire report said not a word about nutritional conditions in the Mukden POW camp itself.

The "cold storage" that Major Peaty referred to was, in fact, nothing more than an ordinary wooden storage shed, where corpses were placed. The prisoners, who had not lost their sense of humour, referred to it as 'Ward 13'.

"I was one step away from Ward 13 and maybe the first person to emerge alive from Ward Zero," wrote T Walter Middleton (Mukden POW #402), who narrowly survived the camp hospital. "There were no drugs in the hospital and no one to take care of us.

This was not a place for restoring health – it was a place of death, of waiting for death," he said.

At first, the military hospital in the camp was divided into three areas. The biggest hall was occupied by the ill patients. Most of the patients' conditions deteriorated. The US military doctors had no medicines, so there was nothing they could do. They could only sit by their dying comrades' sides, offering encouragement and heartfelt suggestions.

The middle area was the sanitation area. The prisoners called the final area 'Ward Zero'; it was for the mortally ill POWs, where their final hopes for life came to an end. It was the last station on their lives' journeys. Once the sickest patients were transferred there, they were taken in order to the door, beyond which stood 'Ward 13' – the morgue.

In the frigid air of the north, with the earth frozen hard, the burial of bodies was impossible, and the corpses were placed in that storage shed as though they were cordwood. The door to the shed was not locked, and the howling wind slammed it to and fro. To the POWs in the hospital, the sound was like the tolling of a deathly bell, beckoning to them to point their footsteps towards oblivion.

Two prisoners in reasonably good health were responsible for carrying corpses from Ward Zero to Ward 13. Once, they found a corpse outside the door of Ward 13, naked and frozen solid in a crawling position. They had no idea who had finally brought the body there.

Oliver Allen said: "I served on burial detail. We buried the corpses in a cemetery not far from the camp. It was a Manchu burial ground. I noticed that they left a burial mound after they completed a burial. After a POW was buried, there was only a wooden cross. Because of the cold, we could not bury corpses until spring, when the weather began to warm up. We would light a little fire to warm and soften the earth. Then we would dig and dig. Then we would light another fire and dig again, until finally the entire corpse could be placed in the ground."

Towery said: "Early on, in that first winter at Mukden, a great many prisoners died. Because they could not be buried in the frozen earth, the bodies were placed in storage. In the icy March of 1943, we buried a total of 176 corpses. The frozen bodies of our comrades were laid to rest in an old Manchu family cemetery. Most of them had died within ninety days of our arrival at Mukden. By winter's end, the number of dead had risen to 205, more than 17 per cent of the American POWs in the camp."

# 5

# FREE LABOUR

"THE VAST MANCHURIA is a prodigious producer of corn, soybeans and sorghum. Japanese colonists have thronged into the area, accompanying the Japanese armed forces. Over 14 years, they enslaved the Chinese to carry out back-breaking agricultural cultivation on their behalf. In the fields and villages, Japanese control left a lasting mark. Japanese social order, punitive law and overall systems are all-pervasive. Manchuria has become Japan's most beautiful province." These were the words of Marcel Junod, Tokyo representative of the International Committee of the Red Cross, conveying his impressions as he travelled through northeastern China.

Such unjust enrichments were undoubtedly of great value to the Japanese. Establishing its hold over Manchuria helped Japan to establish and carry out its policies of advancing southwards. Controlling Manchuria provided an essential guarantee of material resources, and it also constituted a huge psychological boost. Moreover, the prisoners of war in the Mukden POW camp were not only spoils of war; they were bargaining chips, and they were a free labour force.

Mankind's attitude towards prisoners of war arose from the fiery and bloody lessons of countless wars, gradually becoming more enlightened. In the epoch of primitive humanity, prisoners were either slaughtered or enslaved. In the feudal period, the nobility used them as sacrificial offerings. The current guiding document on this issue is the Geneva Convention on Prisoners of War, signed by 47 governments on 27 July 1929. Japan was one of the signatories, but when the second world war erupted, Japan had not formally entered into the agreement. By that time, Japan, well launched on the road to militaristic aggression, was of the view that entering into international conventions such as this meant the abandonment of its unique superiorities; in other words, that Japan would become the acted-upon power rather than the initiator of action.

Thus, not only was the scale of the second world war without historical precedent; the numbers of POWs exceeded anything in the past as well. Because Japan's military operated far beyond the commitments of international law, the brutal enslavement and inhumanity that they inflicted on POWs find no parallel in history.

On 25 June 1942, Tōjō Hideki, prime minister and minister of the army, issued his instructions to the newly appointed POW camp commandants and staffers: "In Japan, we have our own particular view on the handling of prisoners of war. Our approach to their treatment naturally differs from that of the Europeans and the Americans. We must utilise their labour power to the maximum, and whatever expertise they might have, to build up our nation's production, and we have to make every effort to make them assist in our prosecution of the Greater East Asia War. Not a single person is to be wasted."

This kind of bald statement not only makes clear the Japanese strategy of "using war to nourish war", as it was brought to bear on Japan's prisoners of war; it also left the responsibility of how to maximise the use of prisoners to those responsible for managing them.

In September 1942, Allied intelligence picked up a highly classified electronic message from the Japanese minister of transport to the Department of Maritime Transport. It read as follows:

In light of the present acute national labour shortage, we must urgently make use of Caucasian prisoners of war. We must focus on using all available shipping (including civilian and military ships) for transporting white POWs to Japan on their homeward voyages. All maritime transport department heads shall report monthly on the numbers of people they have shipped (with a special separate report covering prisoners of war with special skills or abilities). All possible methods, such as carrying prisoners on the ships' decks, shall be used for the all-out effort to ship large numbers of prisoners.

Most of the Allied prisoners held at the Mukden camp – like aircraft ground personnel, those trained in militarily useful mechanical skills, army doctors and health personnel – came from skilled backgrounds. American POWs came from the Army, the Air Force, the Navy and the Marines. Within the Army contingent were men from the Army Air Force, the infantry and the artillery forces, as well as communications troops, engineering troops and medics. They thus became the prize selection targets as the Japanese military set about carrying out its orders to scoop up all manner of labour power and special skills.

In the three months from November 1942 to February 1943 that the Allied POWs were confined at Mukden, as large numbers of them perished, a crisis condition prevailed and was difficult to control. Even before the situation in the camp had settled down and the rate of prisoner mortality had become clear, the Japanese were urgently working on moving the prisoners into the factory labour force.

On 22 August 1942, the deputy minister in the Army Ministry wrote to the chief of staff of the Kwantung Army, calling for "using the plans for the Manchu Kosaku Kikai Kabushiki Kaisha, Inc. to expand our ability to outfit our aviation units". Not only did the message lay out detailed plans for the utilisation of POW labour in order to speed the increase in military production; it put on paper Japan's wish that the POWs be put to work immediately. The telegram and the plan itself read like this:

Army Asia Secret Message 3129

22 August 1942

Vice Minister of the Army to Chief of Staff, Kwantung Army

In order to carry out the urgent task of outfitting our air forces, as the attached documents make clear, we must increase production at MKK above current levels. The company must focus on the production of lathes needed urgently for production of aerial weapons, ammunition and aircraft. Particularly required are speciality lathes needed by the Nissan Automotive Production Corporation, which is working to increase production of aviation machine guns and ammunition in order to meet current urgent requirements.

Your Army must put every effort into this.

As a further note, we add that the Army Ministry is currently working very hard to assist in the procurement of precision lathes, which are expected to be manufactured within Japan. Because of the high degree of precision of these machine tools, it would be difficult to procure them in Manchuria.

Draft Plans for the Utilisation of the Manchu Kosaku Kikai Kabushiki Kaisha Company to Increase Production of Urgently Required Aviation Equipment

1. Production for 1942 is planned for 80 units (3 million yen). Production for 1943 should reach 400 units (10.5 million yen). Most of that production will be the responsibility of the Kwantung Armaments Industry Company (a unit of Nissan Automotive Company) and will be used to expand the company's production of large batch orders. The remainder will be assigned to the Manchuria Aircraft Company, the Manchuria Auto Company and other armaments plants.

Note: to date, MKK has not received orders from Manchuria Aircraft and Manchuria Auto. After 1944, further negotiations will take place following the dates laid out in the plan.

2. To carry out this plan, the following measures shall be implemented for the purpose of strengthening cooperation with the Army Ministry and securing its support:

a) By providing technical support and technical guidance on increasing production. Within Japan, those with the highest skills in lathe production shall provide designs, on paper, for lathes to be employed in high-volume production, together with work drawing and detailed standards parameters. Further, they shall provide guidance as production rates are raised.

b) Pursue technological upgrading in accordance with the revised plans for training of core technological personnel. The best lathe-production plants and military arsenals in Japan shall implement retraining programmes for core technology personnel at MKK. For this programme, the Nissan Auto Processing Plant, which boasts the best technical personnel in high-volume production, has already sent nine technicians to MKK to carry out a top-to-bottom retraining programme.

c) The best units within Japan shall transfer to core technical personnel and core line workers the technology for improved production. Thus far, high-volume production technology specialists from Tōyō Machinery have worked with MKK, including eight technicians and 12 core line workers. On this matter, because Tōyō has been designated as a plant requiring labour force readjustments, we have already held discussions and received the necessary permissions from the Health Ministry and the Office of Naval Supervision.

d) Make use of prisoners of war to make up for labour shortages. At present, MKK is facing severe shortages of production workers and needs to increase its labour force immediately. Ideally, production workers could be provided to MKK at once, but that is difficult to carry out in practice. MKK is therefore planning to make use of large numbers of prisoners of war as factory labour. If your army and the Manchukuo authorities have no objection, we will supply all necessary assistance to carry out that programme. The numbers of POWs required are as follows, allotted in accordance with the requirements of the various industrial areas:

Machinery inspection labour – 65

Forge workers – 30

Heat treatment workers – 25

Design copiers – 50

Lathe operators – 220

Tool cleaners – 100

Cleaners – 100

Draftsmen – 150

Machine installers – 100

Welders – 20

Wood form workers – 20

Turret lathe operators – 30

Drill lathe workers – 20

Grinding machine workers – 110

Drill lathe workers – 50

Design workers – 80

Buffer workers – 40

Form buffers – 20

Milling machine workers – 85

Gear workers – 45

Carpenters – 10

Electrical equipment installers – 30

Electric generation machinery workers – 20

Machinery technology personnel – 80

Total – 1500

e) Assistance with operating assets. With regard to operations assets, our task will be to try as hard as we can to expand the assets needed for production in Manchukuo. Thus, as we look at this, with regard to machine tools destined for final shipment to Japan, the Army Ministry will provide most of the raw materials.

f) Assist in procuring precision machine tools. MKK's current levels of production equipment for machine tools are far from adequate. Currently, the company's most serious bottleneck is the lack of a variety of precision machine tools. These deficiencies must be remedied. But, whether now or in the future, the company will not be capable of producing precision machine tools on its own. To a great extent, they will remain dependent on help from the best enterprises in Japan. We will therefore offer all assistance in providing these items to MKK. Furthermore, we will ask the military attaché's office of our embassy in Germany to work on ways to assist MKK with importing precision machine tools from Germany on a priority basis. The company will provide a list of items for procurement in accordance with trade procedures established by the Japanese and German governments.

3. Assist Manchuria Aircraft and Manchuria Auto with securing precision machine tools from Japan. Manchuria Aircraft and Manchuria Auto have not yet submitted their purchase orders or formulated specific plans. Most machine tools (especially high-precision machine tools) are currently needed by machine tool plants within Japan. With respect to increasing the capacity of more ordinary plants producing military items, meeting the needs of aircraft manufacturing plants for large numbers of precision machine tools needs to be a high priority. We must do everything possible to avert the damaging effects that the two companies' declining production levels will have on MKK itself.

The requests the two companies have already transmitted to Japanese mainland machinery plants for milling machines and grinding machines are as follows:

Manchuria Aircraft – 120 machines

Manchuria Auto – 260 machines, of which 114 are to be borrowed from army stocks

With implementation of these plans, we can anticipate that increases in MKK's production capacities and technological standards will go far towards meeting the needs of Manchuria Auto and Manchuria Aircraft in the future.

Telegraphed Response of the Chief of Staff of the Kwantung Army to the Deputy Minister of the Army

Asia Secret Document 7991

Secret telegram sent 9 September, 6.20pm and 11.10pm

To: Deputy Minister

From: Chief of Staff, Kwantung Army

Kwantung Army Chief of Staff Message 710

Regarding your instructions on the utilisation of MKK for the rapid expansion of aircraft production, using 1,500 prisoners of war will make up for the shortage of technical personnel in Manchuria in executing these plans. We are opening a POW camp. Please respond quickly with the date of arrival and the number of POWs arriving. We are building the camp to be ready for the POWs this winter, and hope that they will arrive in Manchuria at the earliest opportunity.

P.S. We are expecting your further notice on matters regarding the establishment of the POW camp in the near future.

With regard to the idea of using POWs in carrying out the 'Plan to Utilise MKK for the Purpose of Meeting the Urgent Needs for Equipment in the Aircraft Manufacturing Industry', the Kwantung Army presented the following specific responses:

Date of Telegram: 29 September 1942

To: Chief of the Military Affairs Bureau

From: Chief of Staff, Kwantung Army

Kwantung Army Chief of Staff Message 746

We have now established a prison camp (the Northern Big Camp) at Mukden to house 1,500 prisoners of war sent from the south and will be working this winter to make it a permanent facility. Work will be completed next spring. In view of this, we request the immediate transfer of prisoners.

P.S. We hope for clear instructions from the central organisation with regard to the treatment of the POWs. We will report further details after the prisoners have been received.

All of these telegrams and plans seem to represent concrete evidence of the policy of "using the war to nourish the war". More deeply, they reveal the essential nature of a war built on plundered labour resources.

In his diary, Major Peaty wrote:

13 December 1942: A list prepared of able-bodied mechanics in camp, with a view to starting them at work on the 16th.

21 December 1942: Two Americans died in hospital. 68 mechanics and 187 semi-skilled men went to work at Manchu Kosaku Kikai Kabushiki Kaisha (henceforth known simply as "M.K.K.").

23 February 1943: Funeral service for 142 dead. 186 have died in 105 days, all Americans.

The Japanese troops arranged the POWs in line to go to work every morning at 7am. Labour began at 8am. The prisoners assigned to work in plants outside the confines of the camp were subject to special physical inspections as they left the camp and when they returned to it. They were strictly forbidden to carry contraband from, or into, the camp.

52

One of the prisoners had to walk more than eight kilometres each day to work at MKK. He was already physically depleted, and this long trek was very hard on him. The freezing wind howled about the marching men, making it hard to move ahead. The prisoners felt as though they were on the Bataan Death March all over again. Soldiers with swords stood on both sides of the men. At the rear of the marchers rolled a Japanese military truck, loading up those men who could no longer walk.

"I got to Mukden on November 11th, and started working on December 21st," wrote the American survivor Joseph Vater. "I walked five miles each day to MKK. The weather grew colder and colder. Many of the men had dysentery; you can imagine their physical condition. This plant was established by Americans before the war. I think it was designed by Ford. All the equipment in the plant was made in the U.S.A. All nuts and bolts were to the American standard. Even the signs in the plant were American-style, not made in Japan."

MKK was established around 1940. Its main task was the manufacture of machinery used in the production of other machine tools. Four American engineers were assigned to design and build the workshops. After the war erupted, the Americans left, before the machinery had been fully installed. So, when the American POWs arrived at the Mukden camp, their task was to pick up the construction of this unfinished factory. The first task was to install all the mechanical equipment according to the blueprints.

American survivor Smith Merrill (Mukden POW #276) recalled that, when the POWs first arrived at the plant, they saw that their work assignments called for the installation of completely new American machinery. "The equipment was the most advanced – I had seen nothing this good on American soil or in the US military," he said. Now, these American POWs were forced to use their own country's advanced equipment to strengthen the Japanese; in their hearts, they could not avoid feeling very bitter. Merrill recalled:

53

"Much of the machinery had already been installed before we got there; our job was to install it and test it. We had a number of draftsmen among us, who were assigned to graphics and drawing jobs. One of the machines was like a metal-cutting machine. The metal raw material was fed into one end of it, and from the other end it produced the specified number of small pieces, such as nuts and bolts. This was why they wanted those of us with engineering backgrounds; they wanted to replicate this machine."

Of course, things did not turn out as they had expected. It was not as simple as making nuts and bolts. The Japanese were no strangers to hardship. They had their reasons for shipping large numbers of prisoners of war from the distant battlefields of the Pacific war to a region they had already occupied for ten years and considered to be their 'great rear area'. Even though these POWs had left the field of military conflict, they had not left the wartime environment; instead, they had become 'alternative' capital; 'alternative' tools for the Japanese military to use in prosecuting their war of aggression. This was the tragic reality that the POWs could not avoid confronting.

Russell Grokett was assigned to work at MKK in aircraft parts processing. Grokett was a lathe operator. On one occasion, the Japanese handed him a drawing and ordered him to produce components according to the drawing. Using the skills he had learned maintaining machinery during his military service and his familiarity with military industrial products, Grokett realised that the parts he was supposed to produce would be used in the landing gear of Japan's 'Zero' fighter plane; that they would be used by the Japanese to make war on his own country. That was unbearable for him.

At first, the main job for the POWs was assembling 89 brand-new machine tools. To form the foundations for the machinery, they had to excavate deep trenches in the floor of the plant's workshops and then pour concrete into them. Allen said: "I took part in

54

building the foundations. They ranged in width from 8 to 19 feet, and in depth from 6 to 8 feet. They were extremely long. This was a planing machine, and its pedestal was very long. It required a very heavy foundation. The Americans got the job building the foundation and poured in the concrete – in that way, the base grew deeper and deeper."

A number of Chinese worked alongside the Americans. The Americans discovered that these fellow workers were not very active. "We could not tell whether it was because they could not understand how to install the American machines, or because they just didn't want to see these advanced machines put to work in the hands of the Japanese. If it was the latter, who wouldn't have had the same feelings?" said Allen.

On 19 February 1944, Thomas H Brister (Mukden POW #898) was working at MKK when he was crushed against a pillar by an electric cart, seriously injuring his right leg. The first signs of gangrene appeared on the 21st. Although the camp commandant said that every effort should be made to treat him, the camp hospital lacked medicines and was completely without surgical instruments or an operating room. On the 23rd, Brister succumbed to the high fever induced by the gangrene.

Towery recalled: "In my early days working at MKK, I was working on the construction of a manufacturing building at the plant, carrying bricks up the scaffolding. The higher the building rose, when I stood atop the scaffolding I could see farther and farther beyond the walls of the plant. I could see a world of freedom. Every time I went up there, I lingered a little bit longer. But I was crystal clear: under Japanese control, the Chinese outside the wall were no more free than I was inside. We were all people with no freedom."

In the spring of 1945, Rosendahl and several of his mates were sent to work in the fields outside the camp. "We were to plant corn. The land had been a cemetery. The Japanese overturned the graves and planted the land to crops. A Chinese fellow used a horse and plough, and I did the watering. We worked there throughout every blazing summer day," he said. Rosendahl tried to speak to the Chinese man, who used his hands to try to communicate. What he got across to Rosendahl was that they should not communicate: the Japanese could smash his head. "This Chinese guy's situation was no better than mine," Rosendahl said. "Only, in the evening, he had a home to go to, and I had a prison camp."

Major Peaty had this to say about the POWs' rates of attendance at MKK:

13 January 1943: The factory detail has dropped to 330 due to colds, fatigue, etc.

25 January 1943: 101 more men detailed for work at M.K.K. Attendance averages 60%. Today, there was an inspection by a General of the Japanese Medical Corps.

8 February 1943: 407 men went to the factory – the highest number yet.

4 March 1943: 570 men went to work today. 96.6% of the number allocated.

Of all the plants around Mukden that made use of forced labour by Allied prisoners, MKK used the most. MKK mainly produced aeroplane parts. The Allied prisoner labourers made up the most important part of the plant's labour force. Statistics from 1944 show that the plant had 331 Japanese, 620 Chinese and 500 POWs.

Later on, the Japanese military set up three 'dispatch camps' and two 'branch camps' directly under the control of the main Mukden POW camp. The first of these three dispatch camps, in the Tiexi district of Mukden, served the Manshū Leather Company. The second, in Daxi district, served the Manshū Canvas Company. And the third, in Tiexi district, served both Nakayama Steel and the Tōyō Lumber Company. The three dispatch camps handled a total of 455 POW labourers.

As soon as the Allied troops had been taken prisoner, the Japanese set about conducting a detailed investigation of each prisoner's technical background.

Each man had to report his full name, rank, serial number and professional skills. The prisoners were promptly divided into three labour categories – steel, iron and forest products – and then sent to the corresponding dispatch office for labour assignment. The prisoners worked on machinery installation, machinery operation, machinery maintenance or forging of various components. Some were even assigned to critical design studios, where they created blueprints.

The Takai Iron Works (TKK) lay along the east side of the Mukden POW camp. Its principal product was overhead gantry cranes. The plant issued a detailed request for 20 POW workers. Two had to have drafting experience. The other 18 had to have experience either in steelworking or machinery operation.

All these plants were primarily engaged in military production. Manshū Leather produced boots and other leather military gear of Japanese issue. Manshū Canvas mainly turned out tents. Nakayama Steel Works and Tōyō Lumber, located in the same district, supplied steel and wood items for military construction, but also army helmets and other military goods.

Taken together, all of these examples make clear that the primary purpose of erecting this system of forced labour at the Mukden POW camp was to accelerate and maintain Japan's war of aggression.

# 6

# A DEADLY PRISON BREAK

A HUNDRED AND eighty kilometres northwest of Shenyang, deep in the desert near the Inner Mongolian city of Tongliao, there is a village called Liangjiazi, or 'Two Families'. A kilometre southwest of the village, there lies a long sand dune covered with tall grass. The locals call it 'The American Hump'. The name comes from events 75 years ago. How did this remote village end up with a 'foreign' name? What events lie in its background?

The answer is tied up with the Allied prisoners from the Mukden POW camp.

More than 70 years ago, Liangjiazi was a tiny village of about twenty Mongol families. In its remoteness and isolation, no foreigners had ever made an appearance.

The pastoral tribes of the region maintained their traditions and lived simply. But they viewed outsiders with great suspicion, even hostility.

On the early afternoon of 2 July 1943, after the midday hour of rest, most of the able-bodied villagers had returned to the fields. Only the elderly, women and children remained inside the village. At about 2pm, three men with Caucasian features burst into the village, asking for food. These strangers frightened the villagers, but in their kindness the residents provided them with mutton and sheep's milk. Once they had the food, the three men left in haste.

These three people were American escapees from the Mukden POW camp. They chose to risk death in their escape attempt because conditions inside the camp, and the brutality of their prison guards, were no longer bearable. The three escapees were Marine Sergeant Joe B Chastain (Mukden POW #516), Marine Corporal Victor Paliotti (Mukden POW #444) and US Navy submarine sailor Ferdinand F Meringolo (Mukden POW #1125).

The three had made meticulous secret preparations for the escape. They carried with them sixty pounds of dried dog meat, acquired from the wild dogs trapped by the prisoners. They had managed to get their hands on a map of Mukden, which they used to study possible escape routes. They decided to hide first in the unpopulated wastelands, and then make their way 600 kilometres to the Mongolian border, finally crossing from Mongolia into the USSR.

At 10pm on 21 June 1943, the three men left the separate buildings they were living in and came together in an area of sunken ground near the camp hospital. They cut the barbed wire, slipped out of the camp and made their way, under cover of darkness, towards the northwest.

After the escape of the three prisoners, administration of the camp became much more stringent. The prisoner squad leaders in the three barracks the men had inhabited were immediately thrown into solitary confinement for ten days. The rest of the prisoners in those barracks were confined to their bunks for three days with all talking prohibited. Daily rations were cut by a third. The entire camp was shrouded in tension.

Oliver Allen was working in the kitchen of the plant where he was doing forced labour. One of the escapees, Joseph Chastain, had headed the small team of POW workers there. Allen recalled:

"When we learned that three men had escaped and that Chastain was one of them, we were not surprised. He was our team boss, a true American, very dynamic. And he was a Marine sergeant. But on the day before he took off, he was doing his work side by side with us. He had been bodybuilding using stones and other heavy objects. A few of us said privately to ourselves that he was planning to break out."

The British prisoner Major Robert Peaty recorded all this in detail in his diary. He wrote:

23 June 1943: Three men escaped. Undoubtedly the whole camp will suffer as a result of this event. The Adjutant (Ishikawa Tai) came into the camp a few minutes before roll-call, and appears to have made a round of the barracks flourishing a pistol, and also demonstrating his skill with his sword. I did not see his pistol myself, but watched him flourishing his sword about. At first, I thought he was trimming the willow trees, but later I saw that he was putting in some natty footwork, shuffling backwards and forwards, parrying strokes from an imaginary enemy, thrusting, and raising his sword above his head he would slash downwards with it. The piece-de-resistance came when, dropping to one knee, he made a sideways stroke which was evidently intended to decapitate his opponent. I am no judge of sword-play, but I should say that the Japanese two-handed method does not stand one chance in ten against the European style. I suppose all this was intended to impress us, in view of yesterday's escape, but personally I hope the men get through and can make known the scandal of the lack of medical care which was responsible for the deaths of 15% of the American Prisoners-of-War in this camp.

24 June 1943: Questioning in progress. A rope has been stretched around the inside of the camp a few yards from the barbed wire. Notices say that the penalty for crossing the rope is death. The

Superintendent Officer (Miki Chui) delivered a speech to the effect that in order to prevent future escapes, the barracks (i.e. men in each barrack) are to be organized in groups of ten, with one to be appointed as the leader. Then, if one escapes, the other nine are to be punished. Orders were given to make three coffins – obviously a "propaganda" move, as if they had been caught, there would be no need to continue the questioning – asking the other men where they think they have gone. I hope that the Japanese custom of hara-kiri still endures and that Miki and Noda are to be two of the occupants of the coffins: perhaps we should then see some elementary justice in the camp administration.

The three coffins were placed at the entrance to the camp, so that on their return all the M.K.K. workers might see them. This "intimidation" misfired, for the whole camp is laughing. Personally, I think they are quite capable of loading the coffins with stones, and going through all the business of a funeral.

25 June 1943: Barracks 6, 7 and 14 have been sitting at "kiotsuke" all day under an armed guard as a punishment. (One man came from each barracks, so the remaining 90 are punished). No one is allowed to leave the barracks after evening roll-call, until reveille, except to go to the latrine, in which case he must report to the night-guards. The night-guards will be deemed "conspirators" if anyone escapes. Anyone leaving the barracks except to go to the latrine will be shot. All amusements are forbidden until further orders. All food must be eaten on the spot: anyone saving any food will be deemed to be intending to escape. It is amazing to observe the discomfiture of the Japanese: I think they know we are all laughing at them, and that it has got badly under their skin. (Sitting at "kiotsuke" means sitting cross-legged, oriental fashion, and the inmates of the three barracks have to do this for eight hours a day).

29 June 1943: The Commandant made a speech this morning in which he said that he was "deeply mortified by the outrageous action of the inhuman men who dared to escape". He also told us that we must all go about seeking to discover whom we could suspect of escaping, and must report them at once to the Superintendent. He said that we have been trusted with the spirit of Bushido, but that we should now all be treated with the greatest severity. He added that the men who escaped would not be buried in the cemetery with those who had died of sickness, but their bodies would be left where they lay. (This is obviously a prelude to an announcement that the three men have been caught and shot). We all agree that we shall not believe this story unless we see the bodies. I give a word for word copy of the speech.

"It is entirely out of my expectations to see the betrayal, the most outrageous and unfortunate trouble that has been caused recently. Under the vast virtues of His Majesty the Emperor, all the personnel have treated you with sympathy, spirit of Bushido. But the very three escapees that have dared to go against my wishes may well be said to be absolutely inhuman.

"When all of you try to complete your duty and responsibility, peace and welfare will surely be in your hands. In fact we have considered various means, and have intended to consider in future for the benefit of your welfare. But you yourselves have quited your fortune and thrown yourselves into the state of Hell. We will no longer tolerate any trifling trouble and continue to make the strict surveillance over you up to the time when all of you start your life all over again and I am to punish not only one most strictly that should violate the above warning, but one's ten man group that are jointly responsible for one's misconduct.

"Moreover I will never tolerate anyone who speaks tricks, lies or is insolent in his attitude."

By 2 July 1943, the three escapees had been gone for 11 days.

Though they had reached as far as the Mongol village of Liangjiazi, two thirds of their journey to the Mongolian border still lay ahead. But they had already made it through the more densely populated, and thus most dangerous, part of their journey. They moved slowly, but saw few signs of human habitation, and they were in relative safety. They had already eaten all of the dog meat they carried with them from the camp, and so they decided to take a risk by entering Liangjiazi village in broad daylight in search of food. Fortunately, the villagers not only gave them something to eat but prepared other foods for them to take as they continued their journey.

The three men set out again about three in the afternoon. But soon after, they encountered a mounted policeman in the service of the puppet Manchukuo government. The 31-year-old police officer came from a village a few miles northwest of Liangjiazi. He had just left his home and was on his way to the police station.

The strange western faces of the three escapees caught his attention. He dismounted to question them. Unable to communicate across the language barrier, the three POWs tried to speak with their hands, drawing a picture of an aeroplane. Half believing them and half doubting their story, he ordered two Mongol villagers, both 56 years old, to take the three men to the site of the plane crash, to confirm their identity. As they approached a spot about two kilometres southeast of the village, the escapees huddled over their map, while the others watched. Suddenly, the escapees attacked. The policeman was slashed repeatedly in the belly and fell to the ground, badly wounded. One of the two Mongols suffered wounds to his back. The other man, who had been standing a bit to the side tending to the horses, fled back to the village as soon as he saw what was happening.

After this ferocious encounter, the three escapees could not drop their guard. They hid themselves in the heavy undergrowth of a nearby hill, waiting to flee after nightfall. But they could not know that more misfortune awaited them on their route of escape.

As afternoon gave way to night, and the villagers returned from their labours, they heard that some outsiders had killed one of their own. The whole village was aroused. The infuriated villagers thirsted for vengeance. All the able-bodied males took up their farm implements, ordered the women, children and elderly to stay in their houses, and headed out of the village, searching in all directions, following the tracks in the sand. Soon, they converged on the little hill where the escapees had concealed themselves. They knew from the tracks that the three men were hidden in the undergrowth. As night fell, the villagers posted guard all around the hill leaving the three POWs frozen in their peril. Neither side budged in the thicket; no one dared make a false move. Eventually, the villagers smoked the fugitives out of their hiding place and captured them.

About seven that evening, the policeman died of his wounds. The Mongol who had been wounded in the back took many weeks to recover.

In the end, what was the fate of these three escaped POWs, imprisoned for a second time? Major Peaty wrote in his diary:

5 July 1943: It was announced today that the three men have been caught. The Commandant's speech follows verbatim.

"Since that most unfortunate incident which took place not so long ago, the majority of you have been orderly and well-behaved, but those who perform acts of indiscretion have not died out and an attitude of greater honour and that which behoves a service-man and a gentleman is impressed on all. The three who absconded have been apprehended immediately after their taking off and upon questioning their story is that of gross ignorance and stupidness, which even an ungrown child in Japan would be ashamed of. They are proved to have had no sense of duty or obligation to others, and moving towards a mistaken conception of happiness, they have broken the law and not only thrown away their own happiness, but brought trouble and restrictions on the heads of the conscientious, well behaving persons here. They have thrown themselves into a hellish mesh and if anything, I bear them a great pity.

"Our number is small. Small as it is, we are working day and night for your welfare and also as your guardians. Should you attempt to abscond in face of this, you may for a time move out of the locality and escape our watching eyes, but the network outside the fence is perfect and impregnable. It is clear that immediate apprehension is the fate in store. Going over the fence in face of this is stupidity of bestial lowness.

"It is impressed on all parties that serious reflection on this subject and a faith in us as we place our faith in you is required. Make the most of your day by day and enjoy in peace and quiet your life here. In that will lie the basis for our endeavours to place what we can in the way of amusement and recreation before you. Awaken to this and awaken to the fact also that a disorderly unruly will mean only restricting yourselves, tightening the ropes around you in every move."

The three escapees were brought back to the Mukden POW camp on 6 July. The camp survivor Rosendahl recalled: "Mounted troops brought them back to camp, trussed up with ropes. The men were already unable to walk; they were just dragged into the camp. They knew they were soon to die; they were just like bags of stones. They were practically dead; it made no sense to bother shooting them. By the time the three men were brought back to the camp, they were bloodied from head to toe and could barely walk. But one of them was doing something extremely odd. His head bobbed painfully from side to side. He kicked at sticks lying on the ground. The pockets of his pants were turned out, and he was picking through them with his fingers. It seemed to many people that he had gone out of his mind. But later, the POWs figured out that he was sending a message: "No Stick Out Like Sore Thumb". What he was telling us was that because our faces looked so different from the natives', there was no place to hide."

Oliver Allen recalled: "They brought them back to the camp and tied them up at the camp entrance. We had to look at them every day. It was pitiful. But we never beckoned to them; that would have been very bad for us and wouldn't have helped them at all. We could find satisfaction just standing by their sides."

On 30 July 1943, a Kwantung Army military court sentenced the three escapees to death on charges of theft, murder and attempted murder. They were shot to death the next day. Allen recalled: "We heard that the Japanese offered the men blindfolds. Chastain refused, saying: 'I don't want to cover my eyes.' One of the Japanese said to him: 'If all our troops acted that way, we could conquer the entire world.' If we hadn't been POWs, we would rather have stood with men like that."

After the three escapees were returned to Mukden, they went through all sorts of interrogation. The camp guard named Miki was present through all the interrogations and at the executions. Between 5 and 16 September 1946, at the war crimes trials of Matsuda Genji and Kuwashima Joichi, the prosecution presented Miki's testimony. This is what he said:

1. I am thirty years old. I am a graduate in Economics of the Tokyo Imperial University.

2. During my service in the Mukden POW Camp, I beat ten to fifteen prisoners, with my fists or with clubs, or assaulted them with Japanese swordsmanship.

3. On about 23 June 1943, three prisoners – Chastain, Meringolo and Paliotti – escaped from the camp. On about 10 July, they were captured by Mongols in a village near Zhengjiatun. That day, I went to the Kempeitai base to identify them. They were at that

time ill and weak, and their bodies bore many wounds, incurred when the Mongols attacked them with shovels and axes. Their wounds were cleanly bandaged at the Kempeitai base.

I was present at the interrogations by the Kempeitai, for purposes of later research. After receiving instructions from the Kwantung Army Military Law authorities, we brought the three men back to the Mukden camp and conducted an on-the-scene inquiry into their escape. That was about 20 July.

During the investigation of the three prisoners' escape, the camp commandant, I myself, and an interpreter were present. I do not recall who else might have been present. Chastain provided a detailed account of the escape, so that, as he put it, others would be dissuaded from attempting to escape in the future. He offered his own ideas on what we could do to prevent similar escapes.

Later, I learned that the military trial had sentenced the three men to death because, having killed the Mongol policeman, they were common criminals. I was present at their trial and heard their confessions to having killed the Mongol policeman and wounded one of the local militia. I personally observed their battered helmets and the lids of their food boxes, which had been burned at the time of their capture. I also saw the burned dagger that the policeman had been carrying, which Chastain was carrying at the time of his capture.

On 31 July, the death sentence for the three men was carried out at the POW cemetery. In addition to myself, the camp doctor was present. I represented the head of the Camp, who was, as I remember, ill at the time. Also present were the chief of the Mukden Independent Guard Unit, the chief of the Kempeitai Detachment, three military law officials, a first lieutenant medical man sent by the Kwantung Army, the head of the Penal Detachment (a lieutenant sent from the Independent Guard Unit) and six soldiers who formed the firing squad.

The faces of the three men were covered with white cloths,

and their eyes were blindfolded. Their wrists were fastened to wooden crosses, and they were forced to kneel. The firing squad knelt at a distance of seven or eight metres and took aim. One of the soldiers was to aim at the head, and another at the heart. When the squad leader issued the order, six rifles burst out.

Small amounts of blood appeared on the blindfolds and the clothing of the executed men. After the bodies were inspected by the medical officer sent from the Kwantung Army, the corpses were turned over to camp authorities. We placed the bodies in caskets and buried them in the POW cemetery. I remember that, at the moment of burial, one of the army soldiers from the camp presented a wildflower to each of the coffins, saying: "After death, there is no guilt. Go peacefully to your places in heaven."

A US Army medical doctor and Mukden POW by the name of Herbst kept a diary of his time at the Mukden camp, and in it he recorded the names of all who died there. Along with the prisoner numbers of the deceased, the times of their deaths, the causes of their deaths and the places of their deaths, he recorded the names of the POW medical personnel who certified their deaths. The three escapees were recorded with all the others, but in their cases there was a difference: no US Army medical figure was on hand when they died. Instead, the witnesses were listed as "execution team".

The US medical officer Shabart recalled: "After the Japanese shot the three men, they turned the bodies over to us for burial. We discovered that the place where we were burying them was right next to a Chinese tomb. The whole thing was terribly painful."

Joseph A Petak (Mukden POW #695) said: "The execution of the three prisoners hurt us terribly. In our hearts we grew to hate the Japanese even more. We all harboured thoughts of vengeance against the enemy. These executions not only led us to slack off at work – we began to express our resentments by more and more little acts of sabotage. We couldn't abide this kind of unfair judgement, which was so much in contempt of the Geneva Accords."

That was the origin of the name 'The American Hump' at the village of Liangjiazi. After the incident, the villagers learned that the killers had been Americans. Women in the village would frighten their crying children by referring to it. But the villagers were completely ignorant about who these Americans really were, and why they had come to the village. If they had known at the beginning that these Americans were Allied soldiers, maybe they would have let them go. Years later, when they knew that these Americans had been prisoners of war, and especially after they had learned that the men had been executed by the Japanese, the residents of Liangjiazi village came to understand with regret how mistaken they had been.

# 7

# SECRET FRIENDSHIPS

INSIDE THE CAMP, totally isolated from the world, the endurance of the Allied prisoners of war faced two major challenges. Faced with constant pain and death, they could not see any brightness. The future was beyond their vision. Buried in their desolation, their souls yearned for any kind of consolation. The sympathy and courage of their Chinese fellow labourers helped to give them the will to live. The prisoners, in a strange land far from home, came to understand the deep, warm sentiments of these people from an Allied nation.

Little by little, the POWs working in the factories came to make friends with the Chinese workers in their plants. Whether these Chinese labourers were there to support their families or because they had been conscripted, the only difference between them and the POW workers was that, at the end of the day, they could return to their homes.

In those days, life was very hard for the Chinese people, who were on the borderline between life and death. *The Gazetteer of Shenyang City* records that the monthly per capita grain allowance for ordinary Mukden residents was nine kilograms for adults in

1944. Chinese were forbidden to buy rice; violators were punished as 'economic criminals'. Many Chinese families, without any money to spare, could not buy food. To assuage their hunger, some used what little money they had to buy food of the worst quality.

Major Peaty wrote in his diary:

> Though our food was low in calorific value and lacking in vitamins, so that deficiency diseases were prevalent, yet we had more to eat than the civilian population: everything was rationed, and the quantities the Chinese received were pitifully small. We were hungry, but they were starving.

In the autumn of 1943, the American POW Roland Kenneth Towery was sent to MKK to work. There, Towery not only had many opportunities to encounter Chinese people and learn a little about what was going on in the outside world; he also made friends with Ge Qingyu, someone he came to learn from and care deeply about.

Ge Qingyu was a guard at MKK. Every morning, after the Japanese had conducted body searches of all the Allied POWs, Ge Qingyu took the prisoners from the camp to their various workstations inside the MKK plant. On the way, Towery would try out the little bits of Chinese he had been learning by talking to Ge Qingyu. Simple phrases like *ding hao!* (in those days, a common expression, meaning 'very good'; today, it conveys strongly the feeling of that long-gone era) and *da bizi* ('big nose') became the foundations of a friendship. Little by little, the warm feelings between the two men deepened. Ge Qingyu got his hands on an English-Chinese dictionary to help grow the new friendship. He became the 'interpreter' in the relationship between the two. In this way, Towery and Ge Qingyu became 'friendly co-workers'.

Towery's team was first assigned to work on Building One of

the plant's workshops. Next, he was assigned to work on disassembling and die-making machinery.

Their first task was to take apart a brand-new piece of equipment very carefully and give all the disassembled parts to the drafting team, so that the drafters could create complete blueprints with which to reverse engineer the apparatus.

Because the new machine was made in the US, this was the only way for the Japanese to proceed to make many copies of the original item. Once the blueprints were completed, Towery worked on reassembling the machinery, which was then sent on to another location.

Towery had the chance to pass some of the disassembled bearings on to Ge Qingyu, who took them outside and sold them. Then he brought Towery some things to eat. Towery recalled: "That machinery wasn't very useful with its missing bearings, but they never did figure out what the problem was."

The exchanges between the two men were completely secret. Ge Qingyu would put eggs or other edible items in a prearranged place, like a pile of sawdust, and once Towery got word, he would edge over towards it.

This kind of underground 'trade' was extremely dangerous. Ge Qingyu's workplace was a little shed on the factory grounds. No prisoners were allowed in without permission. Towery once walked into that room, probably to bring some bearings to Ge and take away some food. Suddenly, a Japanese soldier came in. The two men stood dumbfounded. Ge Qingyu was quick on his feet. He picked up a spade and pretended he was showing Towery how to use it. He turned to the Japanese soldier and explained that he was assigning the POW a new task. With that, the Japanese soldier left. Towery realised that this man had helped him at great risk to himself.

Ge Qingyu was also Towery's best source of news, including news of the war and the Allies' gradually growing successes.

According to Towery, all of this gave him and the other prisoners the courage to face their hardships.

Towery returned to the US in September 1945, suffering from the tuberculosis he contracted in the Mukden POW camp. "In those days, we did not have the high-efficacy drugs for conquering tuberculosis," he said. "The only remedies we had were bed rest, quarantine and proper nourishment. I spent a total of five years in hospital isolation wards out of the first ten years following my return." Later, Towery had a successful career as a journalist. He won a Pulitzer Prize in 1955 for his report, 'The Case of Compensation for Retired Soldiers: A Systematic Exposé of Massive Fraud'. For the next seven years, he was deputy director and assistant director of the United States Information Agency. Following that, he returned home to Austin in 1976. In 1981, he was appointed by President Reagan (and confirmed by the Senate) to the board of directors of the Corporation for Public Broadcasting. He served ten years as a member of the board and was twice elected chairman of the board.

After he left the Mukden POW camp, Towery was unable to make contact with Ge Qingyu. It was only after the US and China established diplomatic relations at the end of the 1970s that Towery decided to go to Shenyang to try to find his Chinese friend. He wrote to US Ambassador George Bush, seeking his help, but he learned nothing. As US-China relations continued to develop, finding his Chinese friend became a matter of greater and greater urgency for Towery.

In March 2005, Towery sent a photograph of Ge Qingyu to me, along with Ge's address at the time of Towery's imprisonment. I searched far and wide, and finally tracked down Ge's whereabouts. But Ge and his wife had passed away years before. Back at the time of Towery's imprisonment, he had seen an infant less than a year old in Ge's family. The child had died very young. When Towery learned this, he was grief-stricken. By way of remembering his

Chinese friend, Towery developed and printed a number of photographs taken during those years, and sent them to Ge's children. When I visited him in 2007, Towery said: "My heart finally achieved some measure of peace when I was able to deliver those photos of Ge Qingyu into the hands of his children." Towery also sent funds to support the college education of Ge's children. He said: "I hope that this modest and inadequate financial assistance will help the family. And I hope that the friendship of the Chinese and American people can grow stronger on the shoulders of our successor generations."

Robert Rosendahl recalled: "When we were in the camp, we knew nothing about what was happening on the outside. The only reading material the Japanese allowed us to look at was the *Nihon Jihō* (or *Japan Times*) which was in English and published in Tokyo. There was nothing of interest in it, and it was a month or more out of date by the time we saw it. Although the paper was filled with the sayings in the Japanese favour, we could figure out some of the developments in the war. Because the Japanese were endlessly announcing that they were winning the war, we could figure out that the Americans were gradually moving northward."

Because of the news blockade, the prisoners' Chinese co-workers became the most dependable conduit for news. "Late in the war, we heard that big battles were already taking place in the Philippines – that was the best news our Chinese friends brought to us," said Rosendahl. "They managed to tell us news from the outside. All of the POWs working at MKK had their own personal channels." The men used these treasured bits of information from their Chinese informal sources to show off in front of their fellow POWs.

The POW survivor James Bollich worked in one of the wood-processing facilities at MKK. He noticed that Chinese workers continually brought lumber into the plant on horse-drawn wagons and sometimes took wood out of the plant as well. "We were hungry all the time and thought about nothing but eating. One of the wagon drivers gave me a grasshopper to eat. It was so delicious," he said.

The prisoners yearned for things to eat, but they also needed to find places to hide their food. If they tried to bring food back to the camp, the Japanese guards would discover it during their routine meticulous body searches.

Bollich and his comrades soon discovered a spot not far from their wood-processing shop where cement pipes were stacked. They pilfered one of the pipes and covered it over with earth. That was where they stashed the food their Chinese fellow workers managed to give them. In the summer, they covered the pipe with wooden planks, and in the winter the pipe was buried in snow. "We worried about it every day in the camp. Each morning, when we got to work, our first concern was to be sure that the food was still there," said Bollich

Oliver Allen worked in the kitchen at the plant, alongside several Chinese. He recalled that there was one thing in particular that caused him great remorse: "Because he would not divulge the 'bad things' we were doing, Cook Wang lost his job."

In the beginning, the kitchen where Allen worked was different from other kitchens; its only function was to provide meals for the POW workers. But some of the equipment and storage areas were shared jointly with the other kitchens. Great quantities of soybean oil were stored there, for the sole use of the Japanese. The POWs discovered something very interesting behind the barrels of oil. Early one morning, the prisoners intentionally made the air in the kitchen unbearably foul. They heated water to boiling point and removed the lids from their pots. In a minute, the kitchen filled with blinding steam. Under cover of all the smoke and steam, the POWs went into action, using the containers they had brought to steal soy oil from the big barrels and pour it into their own cookers. Wang Shizhuan, standing to the side, saw all this with his own eyes.

Later, the Japanese discovered that their soy oil supplies were too low, and they opened an inquiry. Wang was the head cook in his kitchen, responsible for all the food supplies in the storerooms. If soy oil was missing, he bore the blame. Allen said: "Wang knew exactly what had happened because he was standing right there with us. But he said nothing. I keep thinking about this – he lost his job but said nothing about where the soy oil had gone. We did the deed but still Wang kept quiet. He could have talked." For this, Wang lost the employment that fed his family. Allen said with feeling: "At the cost of his own job, he protected us. That was what Cook Wang did."

At the time of writing this book, Li Lishui was 90 years old. His family hailed from Shen county in Hebei province. After the Sino-Japanese war broke out with the Lugouqiao Incident of 7 July 1937 near Beiping (as Beijing was then known), northern China fell to the Japanese. The Japanese army had already invaded Shen county by 1938. He watched as the Japanese soldiers burned and pillaged and murdered, and the shadow of war covered his soul. Japan's war of aggression brought pain and heavy suffering to every Chinese family. Before all this happened, Li Lishui's father had gone outside the Great Wall, alone, to earn money to support his family. After 7 July, he had no way of making his way back inside the Great Wall, and no way of sending money home to his family. To escape from the chaos of the war, the family entrusted someone to take young Li Lishui to Mukden to take shelter with his father, who was working there. Li's father was working as an electrician in the Mukden Arms Production Facility.

The Mukden Arms Production Facility had formerly been the Northeastern Provinces Arsenal, established under the Chinese general Zhang Zuolin, who controlled the region before 1928. In scale, technical standards and production capacity, it was one of China's top-ranking weapons production units. After the 18 September Incident in 1931, the Japanese Kwantung Army seized the arsenal and renamed it the Mukden Arms Production Facility.

The plant became the most important supplier of guns and ammunition to the Kwantung Army. The arsenal included shops making rifles, artillery, bullets and artillery shells, as well as a machine shop and a gunpowder works. At its peak, the workforce numbered 30,000.

In those disordered days of chaotic armed conflict, a chance to work at a place like the Mukden Arms Production Facility was a golden opportunity. When Li Lishui first arrived, his father hoped that the boy could find work there, as he himself had managed to do. Because the boy was so young, he was assigned only the lowly job of 'miscellaneous labour', running errands and doing odd jobs. After a year, Li Lishui became an electrician's apprentice.

Father and son worked together at the same place. Their situation was good. But life is hard to understand sometimes. Because the father had kicked a Japanese trainee in the plant, he angered his Japanese foreman. To avoid a catastrophe, he had no choice but to leave the Mukden Arms Production Facility and transfer to MKK. In 1942, Li Lishui's mother and younger brother arrived from their home, south of the Great Wall, and the entire family lived together in Mukden. In the same year, Li Lishui transferred over to MKK and started work as a journeyman machinist.

Li recalled: "A lot of Allied POWs were working at MKK, mainly in the Number One and Number Two shops. Those were the two biggest workshops in the entire plant. They were at least double the size of ordinary factories. They were equipped with the most modern machines." Although Li Lishui's Number Three shop was only ten metres from Number One and Number Two, no Chinese workers were allowed into the shops where the POWs were working unless they had special reason to be there. Particularly after the escape incident, rules like this were rigorously enforced. Anyone with no particular connection who casually engaged with the POWs was risking his own life.

The POWs were labouring in another workshop, but Li Lishui frequently had a chance to see one prisoner who bore the number 266. He could see 266 working on a scraping machine, and concluded that he must be a grinder worker. But from time to time, 266 was cleaning up and worked his way to the very doorstep of Li Lishui's shop. After a while, this Chinese worker figured out that the other man was a prisoner of war, and his feelings of sympathy grew.

Every time the two men encountered each other, they would carefully exchange friendly greetings, using only their eyes, because the Japanese forbade any Chinese from having contact with the POWs unless there was a special reason.

One day, Li Lishui and Zhang Liancai, a fellow worker of Li's age more or less, were singing while taking a break. A horse-drawn wagon cart passed by, laden with vegetables on its way to the factory kitchen. Seeing such a rich load of tomatoes and cucumbers, Li and Zhang crept forwards until they were just behind the cart. Li snatched a couple of cucumbers, and Zhang grabbed some tomatoes. Then they dropped back, as though nothing had happened. Once they had fallen behind, the two men squatted in a corner to eat their trove.

Just at that moment, Li Lishui had the feeling that someone was watching him. He turned his head, and there was Number 266, not far off, watching him and Zhang. Li could see the desperate hunger in 266's eyes. No Japanese were in sight. Li softly tossed a couple of cucumbers to the ground in 266's direction, and with his eyes said: "This is for you." Number 266 got the friendly message and used his broom to bring the cucumber towards him. He bent over and picked up the cucumber, but instead of eating it, he hid it in a nearby toolbox. Then he went on with his cleaning, as though nothing had happened.

All that had happened so many years before. Li Lishui had never learned the name of Prisoner 266.

In 2001, I visited Li Lishui and heard this story. We sifted through all the clues relating to Prisoner 266 and finally made a contact in the US. Early in 2002, Li Lishui finally learned Prisoner 266's identity: Neil Gagliano, a soldier in the US Army Corps of Engineers' 803rd Detachment.

Ninety years old by that time, Gagliano clearly remembered the cucumber incident and, through an intermediary, he sent Li Lishui a message of profound thanks for taking the risky step of offering those very special cucumbers.

The prison escape in the summer of 1943 ended tragically with the capture of the escapees and their execution at the hands of the Japanese. The ensuing investigations continued without end. The most intensive inquiry sought to determine where the escaping prisoners had got their hands on their two maps.

One morning, just after work had begun, the Japanese called all Chinese workers together in the factory courtyard. They brought out the three captured escapees and ordered them to identify the Chinese workers who had provided the maps. Li Lishui was standing in the crowd of assembled workers. But Li saw that the three POWs were feeble and dazed; no Chinese worker was named. Nevertheless, a little later, word circulated among the Chinese workers that one of their number had links to the escaped POWs and that the Japanese had arrested him. The word was that this Chinese labourer was named Gao Dechun.

Gao Dechun was an honest Mukden man, one of a few men in the plant responsible for training apprentices. Next to the signboard with MKK's name on it, there was another sign that read, 'MKK Youth School'. This was a special school for increasing the plant's resources of technically proficient mechanics.

All of the trainees in the school were Japanese. At the school, they learned machining and went into the plant for fixed periods of practical training. Gao Dechun was one of those responsible for training the MKK Youth School students in the plant's workshops.

Twenty POWs were assigned to work under Gao Dechun, and he oversaw their work assembling the machines. Each morning, the POWs would exchange friendly greetings with him. Despite their age difference, Gao would respond each day with a hearty "Good Morning!"

A number of Japanese Youth School trainees were also in Gao's team. One day, one of the young Japanese came rushing up to Gao Dechun, shouting at him to get up. Gao had no idea what had happened, but he could see that the Japanese was upset about something. They couldn't communicate with each other. Gao was of a naturally unyielding disposition. In the end, he threw a punch at the Japanese student, who was putting on an arrogant display.

Just as the puppet government of Manchukuo was nominally headed by a Chinese person, the nominal boss of the MKK plant was Chinese. But the real power lay with the number two figure in the company, who was Japanese. Gao knew that hitting a Japanese person meant big trouble, so he raced to report the incident to the management. The Japanese student arrived soon after, claiming that Gao Dechun had struck him. The Japanese manager simply could not imagine that a Chinese person would hit a Japanese person, and he gave the Japanese trainee a tongue lashing. Gao Dechun had a lucky escape.

But that was not the end of the incident. Later on, Gao Dechun found out why the Japanese trainee had been so angry with him. It turned out that, in the young man's textbook inside the plant, a page with a map had been torn out. When he approached Gao, he had intended to ask what had become of the missing page. Gao knew that hitting the man was wrong, so he went out on the street, bought another map, and stealthily inserted it in the student's textbook in order to calm the Japanese man down. He had not anticipated how much trouble that would cause him.

The investigations that followed the prisoner escape discovered that the escapees' map had come from the textbook in question. Gao

Dechun was called before the Kempeitai for interrogation and tortured brutally. "It was unbearable, the hot pepper water, the kerosene, the rack ..." Gao said, many years later, of those hair-raising tortures. Even as he spoke, he was filled with fear.

In the end, Gao Dechun confessed under the torture that he had given the map to the POWs. The Japanese sentenced him to ten years of hard labour for "opposing Manchukuo and resisting Japan". Gao was sent to the Mukden Number One Prison.

When Japan surrendered on 15 August 1945, Gao's imprisonment of more than two years came to an end, and he regained his freedom. While he was behind bars, however, his family had run into misfortune. With the mainstay of the family gone, his wife fell seriously ill, and her young baby starved to death.

These stories occurred at the Mukden POW camp. They testify to the hardships that the Chinese people endured under Japanese control during Japan's aggressive war. They testify as well to the precious friendships that grew between the POWs and their Chinese co-workers in the midst of terrible tribulation. And they bear witness to the tragic historical reality that, in wartime, lives are devastated, and human rights are recklessly trodden underfoot.

Even as the Allied prisoners of war performed their slave labour under the Japanese, they came to sense the sympathy and recognise the generous help of the Chinese people. For those who survived, Mukden held a special place in their hearts and minds. Neil Gagliano observed: "The time in Mukden was three lost years. For three years, Mukden was our spiritual home."

In the summer of 2005, the American consulate general in Shenyang presented Certificates of Gratitude to the family members of Li Lishui, Gao Dechun and Ge Qingyu, expressing thanks to the three for the help and care that they had offered to Allied prisoners of war, and pledging that the American government and American people would always remember their basic humanity and their courage. In recent years, not a year goes by without a visit by some of the former POWs to Shenyang, where they exchange memories and stories of the time they spent with their Chinese fellow labourers.

If it can be said that "forgetting the past is a form of treachery", we must now never forget how Chinese and Allied armies and civilians stood shoulder to shoulder, facing their common enemy, sharing their common destiny and defending their common interests.

# 8

# RESISTANCE

DURING THE PACIFIC WAR, in places other than Mukden, the Japanese made use of all manner of existing local structures – army bases, prisons, schools – as POW facilities. The Bilibid POW camp in the Philippines, for example, had been a common jail. Mukden was the only facility built from the ground up to house prisoners of war. We might say that Mukden was built to a specific scale, in accord with Japanese calculations of specific numbers of prisoners, and specific forced-labour requirements. The Japanese referred to it as the 'Mukden Prisoner of War Camp', or by the shortened term, 'Main Camp'.

On 29 July 1943, the POWs were transferred from the temporary camp at the 'Northern Big Camp' to a new location, less than a kilometre from the MKK factory, at No. 38, Section 1, Xingmin Street, Dadong District. By the standards of the time, this was a highly specialised POW camp, with the most up-to-date equipment. The camp was heavily guarded. A wall two metres high, topped with high-voltage wires, surrounded the site with a watchtower in each of the four corners.

The Japanese portrayed the new facility, once it was in

operation, as a "model POW camp". Japanese Propaganda Corps showed up regularly to make publicity films. In a three-year period, high-ranking Japanese military officers came on inspection tours twenty times. Of special note, the Japanese permitted the International Committee of the Red Cross to inspect Mukden in 1943, 1944 and 1945. This was virtually unheard of in the Japanese army. Countless IRC requests to inspect Japanese POW facilities had been rejected. Internally, Mukden clearly claimed the attention of the highest levels of the Japanese military, while externally it functioned as a showpiece.

Construction of the new camp began on 6 March 1943. The British Major Robert Peaty wrote in his diary:

6 March 1943: Several American and British officers, and all the barrack-leaders, were taken to Mukden today to witness the ceremony of digging the first sod for the new barracks which is to be erected to house the Prisoners-of-War, at an estimated cost of Y5,000,000. As this was the first time most of us had been outside the camp, the trip in itself was an event of great interest, for it took us through the Chinese quarters of the city. A corpse stripped of clothing laying by the roadside was an unusual sight. The actual ceremony was performed under the direction of a Japanese Shinto priest, who wore robes of great beauty.

10 June 1943: Most of the officers were taken to Mukden to see the new barracks, which are nearing completion.

27 July 1943: Preparations put in hand for our move to the new camp.

The new 'Mukden Prisoner of War Camp' was intended to be permanent and had a capacity of 1,500 prisoners. It occupied 49,301 square metres. The total area of all structures was 13,730 square metres. Barracks and other structures used by the POWs came to 11,550 square metres. There were three two-storey barracks buildings, one two-storey hospital and a POW kitchen; in total, nineteen brick structures including the Japanese headquarters and the various Japanese guard units. Each part of the camp had clearly defined functions, giving it a high degree of specialisation.

Here is how Major Peaty described the move to the new camp:

29 July 1943: We moved to the new camp today. When we got there, each man was thoroughly searched. The barracks are a step up. But the four-metre wall topped with high-voltage wire leaves us with the powerful feeling of confinement. At least, in the old camp, we could still cling to the thought that we might again have our lives.

30 July 1943: The new barracks have water pipes and taps but thus far there is no water. For three days we have had only bread to eat, because the stoves from the old camp have not yet arrived, but the new kitchen is supposed to be completed soon. Our personal possessions are still being searched, but we are not allowed to be present. Personal items such as photos of our mothers or wives have been confiscated and destroyed by the guards. Actions like this can only generate more hatred.

To the Japanese, this new prison camp merited the designation as a 'model camp'. Peaty said it was a propaganda camp:

We received so many visits from the Japanese Propaganda Corps, who brought cine-cameras and took reels of baseball games, the men marching to work (with all Japanese guards well out of sight), quizzes, spelling-bees, camp orchestra and sing-songs, service at Christmas time, and so on and so forth.

It is clear from Peaty's diary that the Japanese had put a lot of thought into this 'model camp':

22 July 1943: Special holiday "with amusements" for the benefit of the Propaganda Corps, who took photos and recordings of a concert, baseball and a memorial service held at the cemetery, organized by the Japanese camp staff.

14 November 1943: The Propaganda Corps arrived again.

2 April 1944: The Propaganda Corps is back again. Everyone was ordered to write a 150 word radiogram, or state his reason in writing for not doing so, and some of these messages were recorded.

25 August 1944: Inspection by a visiting General. An American was given 20 days detention this morning for striking a factory guard. We are told that the Red Cross parcels will be withheld if this occurs again, and are threatened with the prohibition of all recreation if we do not write radiograms for the Propaganda Corps.

26 August 1944: Propaganda Corps making recordings of our band, and so on.

27 August 1944: Propaganda Corps recorded a certain number of messages home, and quizzes etc.

The Pacific war of the 20th century was the most vicious conflict in the history of humanity. Human nature was annihilated. Misery gripped existence itself. Chaos ruled. In wartime, the warring parties do not conduct normal foreign relations. Any necessary foreign-policy documents between them must be passed back and forth by neutral third-party nations. For example, on 27 December 1941, the US sent an enquiry to Japan through the Swiss government, asking whether Japan would treat prisoners of war in accordance with the Geneva Convention. Japan replied on 29 January to say that it had never ratified the Geneva Convention, so "although not bound by the Convention relative to treatment prisoners of war, Japan will apply *mutatis mutandis* provisions of that Convention to American prisoners of war in its power". The British government sent a similar message to Japan through the Argentine government on 3 January 1942 and received a similar Japanese answer on 29 January.

For this reason, the only organisation capable of operating among the combatants in wartime, the International Committee of the Red Cross, opened up large-scale and difficult operations to protect the wellbeing of prisoners of war. In Europe, the IRC inspected POW camps and brought packages of essentials for the prisoners. It handled incoming and outgoing mail for the prisoners as well. But in Asia, the IRC encountered unheard of difficulties in trying to negotiate with Japanese authorities.

The International Committee of the Red Cross began in 1863 as a private organisation headquartered in Geneva. Its central mission was to provide humanitarian assistance to people trapped in extreme and life-threatening emergency conditions. Its founding principles were neutrality, fairness, independence and non-interference in political affairs. Through years of international consolidation, by the outbreak of the second world war, the IRC had become an important international body, especially after its promotion of the Geneva Convention on the Treatment of Prisoners of War (known for short as the Geneva Convention) in 1929. The convention aimed to establish fundamental principles of conduct among nations with respect to prisoners of war or others in situations of humanitarian crisis. The convention became an important foundation of international law.

According to the Geneva Convention, each wartime combatant was supposed to select a neutral nation to serve as its 'protector state', to handle its interests within enemies' boundaries. The protector state was empowered to visit and hold private conversations with prisoners of war from the country with which it was affiliated. Article 87 of the convention stated that combatant nations could not interfere with the humanitarian work of the International Committee of the Red Cross, and emphasised the IRC's importance. It held that a firm mastery of prisoner-of-war conditions was of value in negotiations among the parties and in mediation efforts. Nevertheless, though it was thus protected by international law, the International Committee of the Red Cross faced huge obstructions by the Japanese government as it attempted to carry out its work.

In the early stages of the Pacific war, the number of Japanese prisoners taken by the Allied forces was small – much smaller than the number of Allied troops captured by the Japanese. For that reason, Japanese officialdom took no notice of the IRC's work. The Japanese military did not recognise the representative offices of the IRC in Thailand, Singapore, Java, Sumatra, the Philippines and Borneo. It recognised only the IRC representative offices in Japan, Shanghai and Hong Kong. Without legal foundations, the work of the IRC in Japanese-occupied territories was extremely dangerous. In Borneo, for example, the husband and wife representing the IRC were executed by the Japanese army as 'spies' after they tried to assist POWs there.

We know from several historical documentaries what was in the 'aid packets' distributed by the IRC all over the world: food, cigarettes and some basic sanitation and health items. These IRC packets not only gave prisoners of war some needed material items; even more importantly, they were a comfort to the prisoners and helped to raise their spirits.

After the outbreak of the second world war, the IRC gathered as many as 27 million packets for distribution worldwide. The packets came from the UK, the US and Canada. In Europe, their distribution went relatively smoothly. In Japanese-occupied regions of Asia, however, distribution was blocked. In August 1942, Japan announced that the ban on neutral ships' entrance into Japanese-held territories only extended to ships flying the IRC banner. This effectively meant that IRC packets could not be delivered to any prisoners of war. From September 1943, IRC packets piled up on the docks of Vladivostok. The Japanese argued that any ships bearing the aid packages would be sunk by the Allies.

Because of its location, a small number of IRC packets reached the Mukden POW camp by land. Though these packets could not fully relieve the camp's shortages of drugs, food and clothing, they gave spiritual nourishment to the POWs, as expressions of the international community's concern for them.

As for correspondence, only a tiny number of prisoners were permitted to write to their immediate family members, and their letters all had to pass Japanese censorship. The correspondence was long delayed. On 15 August 1945, the day the camp was liberated with Japan's surrender, 65 bags of mail, almost all of it sent from the other side of the Pacific two years before, were discovered. Even the IRC representative office's correspondence had to undergo repeated searches as it passed through Tokyo. Major Peaty, the British prisoner, wrote:

16 July 1943: 20 thirty-five work radiograms were submitted for transmission by Radio Tokyo. The big event of the day has been the signing of the letters we wrote in May. The Japanese seem a little touchy about the number of letters we are allowed to write, as they deleted the mention I made of it in mine. I believe that under International Law we should be able to write once a month.

11 January 1944: 466 letters and 15 parcels for Americans. These

letters were posted between 1 July 1943 and 15 September 1943. A short speech was made to the recipients of the parcels, saying that they were not to complain about looting, as the parcels had been opened before arrival here. We have, however, observed that the Japanese officers have been drinking Brazilian coffee during the past three weeks, in the office.

10 September 1944: The first of the long-awaited mail was released today, after being held up for 102 days, 1,150 letters being given out, all from the U.S.A.

1 March 1945: The Americans received several letters today, and one of the interpreters is reported to have said that they were censored a year ago. We do know that mail arrived at the same time as the last Red Cross consignment. The Camp staff gave the impression that there is some regulation which limits the number of letters that may be given out at one time. The total number given out on this occasion was 2,500. It is now a year since the British received any.

23 March 1945: Five cablegrams were received that others have arrived for us. Some of these cablegrams mention that the senders have been writing every fortnight, from which it appears that some arrangement is in existence with the International Red Cross, whereby mail to us is accepted (and presumably forwarded) at fortnightly intervals. Which makes it all the more strange that so far the British have received no letters addressed to Manchuria at all. Those we have had have all been sent from Korea, which we left in 1942. We opened 120 more parcels today.

8 June 1945: About 1,500 letters were given out, mostly over two years old.

17 August 1945: We got our mail out of the Japanese office, and estimate it at 30,000 letters, which have been untouched for a long time, as many of them have been eaten by rats, and most are two years old. I found twenty-two from my wife, and some from my father-in-law dated July 1942 – over three years old.

Although IRC representatives were specially permitted by the Japanese army to visit the Mukden camp, they were at all times accompanied by officers from the commandant's office. No private conversations with prisoners were possible. It was extremely hard for the IRC representatives to learn much about conditions inside the camp.

On 19 September 1944, the IRC representative in Tokyo, Harry Angst, requested permission to visit the Mukden camp. After a long delay, he finally set out on 6 December. Upon his arrival, he was subjected to strict supervision and restriction. He was accompanied everywhere; not only by a Foreign Ministry official, but also by a staff officer and a lieutenant assigned by the Kwantung Army as his 'companion' on all his inspections. The camp commandant and several officers made their official 'introduction of the situation'. All conversations between the IRC representative and the representative of the inmates had to be observed by the 'companions'. Of more than a thousand prisoners in the camp, the Japanese arranged for only two officers and two enlisted men to serve as prisoner representatives.

Major Peaty, who participated in those talks, wrote:

6 December 1944: A few panes of glass were given out, to replace some of the cardboard, and meat was issued for the first time since 23 November. Both, no doubt, were "window-dressing" for the benefit of the Red Cross representative, Mr. Angst, who came today, with whom Major Hankins and I had an interview in the same circumstances as before. He asked many questions and I

answered less guardedly than last year, as there are so many things needed that a chance had to be taken about reprisals. As regards treatment, I said that it had greatly improved during the past year, as there had not been nearly so many cases of men being beaten up since Lt. Miki left. I am sure that he got the point – that beatings up are still going on, and at the same time, the Japs thought I was paying them a compliment by saying it had improved. Still, that is the way one had to tackle these people. I also asked for dental equipment if possible, and told him that we had received neither dental nor optical treatment since our arrival. Hawkins asked for food and boots, and I asked also for any surgical equipment that could be spared.

Camp survivor T Walter Middleton recalled: "As soon as the IRC team arrived, the Japanese started a performance. Suddenly, we had pork and other good food to prepare in the kitchen. But as soon as the IRC people left, the Japanese took all that for themselves. The visitors naturally had another impression."

After the inspection at Mukden, the IRC's Angst made his 'Report on Inspection of the Mukden POW Reception Facility'. The original, in French, was forwarded to IRC headquarters, to IRC representative offices in the US, the UK and Japan, and to foreign-affairs offices in the respective governments. The report introduced the basic situation in the camp; various camp facilities; time allotted for food, drink, work and rest; care of the sick; compulsory labour; the small store selling minor items; prisoner correspondence, etc. The report was written in a flat style and made no mention of the ill treatment of the POWs.

Looking back, under the conditions established by the Japanese, how could such a report have given a complete picture of conditions in the camp? Did Angst grasp the abuses and the torments the POWs suffered? It all raises a giant question mark. It was no wonder that some of the prisoners not only raised small complaints about details in the report, but doubted the very truthfulness of the document.

On 8 August 1945, after Angst had departed, one of his representatives, Doctor Marcel Junod, arrived at the camp for another inspection. Dr Junod was born in Switzerland in 1904 and had graduated from the surgery department of the University of Geneva Medical School. Starting in October 1935, he had been sent by the IRC on missions to Ethiopia and Spain, to inspect POW facilities, interview prisoners and initiate international aid activities.

What kind of a place was the Mukden camp from Dr Junod's perspective? We can find some answers to that question in his book *Warrior Without Weapons*, written late in his life. He wrote: "We moved by car through an area filled with factories and came up to camp location, surrounded by white walls topped with barbed wire. Watchtowers stood at its four corners." They were taken to the Japanese officers' mess inside the camp, accompanied by the camp commandant Matsuda Genji. Junod recalled: "With both hands on the scabbard of his sword, he sank down into a sofa and urgently asked us to sit." Then, Matsuda spoke to the visitors "like a professor lecturing to his students". First, Matsuda and his colleagues introduced the general situation at the camp, using maps and masses of statistics. More than twenty Japanese officers surrounded them, "some of them were seated on their chairs, continually adding their comments and approving noises". With a great passionate display of admiration, Matsuda "raised his right hand and stamped his feet on the floor". The time allotted for the camp visit was passing quickly, and Junod asked to see the prisoners. Matsuda refused, on the grounds that the prisoners were all at their labours.

Then, Junod was led to the so-called 'hospital' by Matsuda. He described how three or four POWs stood near the window and bowed as they passed. The prisoners who could not stand were sitting on their beds with their legs crossed, and they all refused to look at him directly. Junod described how the prisoners seemed to be reluctant to speak without Matsuda's permission. When Junod boldly questioned an Australian prisoner directly, he only received very brief answers.

Emerging from the hospital, Junod was taken to a storeroom bulging with Red Cross packets. Most of the packages had travelled on a Soviet ship by way of San Francisco, Vladivostok and Busan, Korea, where they were put aboard a Japanese boat and shipped to Mukden. One can imagine Junod's anger, seeing these masses of aid packages intended for the POWs who had suffered so much deprivation, stacked in a storeroom by the Japanese.

Then, Junod and his party went to inspect the cemetery in the northern suburbs of Mukden. In his memoirs, Junod said there was a tall white wooden cross at the top of the cemetery, with many smaller crosses arranged in rows around it. The Allied POWs made garlands of Chinese wildflowers, and the accompanying Japanese officer helped to make a wreath. Junod observed that the Japanese were "ruthless to the living, but have infinite awe of the dead". As he walked along the crosses, he silently read the names of more than 200 deceased prisoners.

At the end of their tour, after a great deal of negotiating, Junod and his party had a chance to see General Wainwright. Junod described how Wainwright and a group of other prisoners stood motionless and then immediately bowed their heads when Matsuda's sword hit the floor. Junod found it hard to watch this humiliation.

After a brief and rudimentary conversation, the Japanese ushered Junod out, ending the interview. He wrote in annoyance: "After so much suffering and tribulation, and after spending the last two months simply getting to Mukden, our conversation was over in two minutes."

Angst's report and Junod's memoir both form a record of the history of the Mukden POW camp. The former was an official report, describing reality through the use of data and statistics. The latter was a private individual's perspective, exhibiting much greater sympathy and understanding. But in both cases, humanitarian investigation under the scrutiny of the Japanese was bound to be constrained. The words of neither of these men conveyed the brutality of the Japanese treatment of their prisoners.

After the war, the Military Tribunal for the Far East, during the debate over the "summary conclusions with regard to the prisoner of war question" and the appropriate sentences for Class A war criminals, the defence used the IRC report on the Mukden inspection as the foundation of their case. They claimed that health, living spaces, food and clothing at the camp were all fine. They went so far as to claim that the Mukden prisoners had experienced no ill treatment and that whatever adverse conditions they might have suffered were the result of wartime material shortages. The good conditions the prisoners experienced, the defence claimed, resulted from the relatively light shortages of material and medical supplies. The aggressive war launched by the Japanese militarists caused terrible destruction in China's neighbouring countries. But at the international court, they used excuses about economic stagnation to explain their own criminal behaviour. What perverted logic!

Really, it was a gigantic joke!

# 9

# THE ANGRY BULL

INSIDE THE MUKDEN CAMP, the Japanese maintained a system of special punishments – solitary confinement, collective detention and so on – to humiliate and intimidate their prisoners. These harsh concepts of prisoner management had their roots in the Japanese traditional spirit of Bushidō – the Way of the Warrior. A core principal of Bushidō is that death is preferable to surrender, and that surrender is the worst shame that can be brought upon nation, family and individual. In the view of the Japanese, death in battle was the highest form of glory.

On the surface, the fact that Japan had not ratified the Geneva Convention was the root of its forced-labour system and its abuse of prisoners of war. This distorted Japanese-style conception of POWs had much deeper foundations in the realm of ideas. Tōjō Hideki, who served as prime minister and army minister at the time, remarked: "To live as a prisoner of war is to live without a shred of honour." This was the polar opposite of western conceptions of the dignity of life. William E Brougher (Mukden POW #1599) wrote in his memoir: "In their concepts of war, the chasm between the Americans and the Japanese is huge and unbridgeable. There is no better proof of this than the respect with which we Americans regard the POWs."

For this reason, the Allied POWs at Mukden faced more than the problems of inadequate food and medical supplies or cruel treatment. What was even worse was the utter lack of recognition of, and respect for, their identities as human beings. The prisoners – enlisted men or generals, young or old – had to be extremely careful, lest they bring down a savage beating by their guards.

In his 'Report by a Prisoner of War on Conditions in Manchuria' in December 1945, Major Peaty summed up in this way:

Beatings were of such frequent occurrence that one ceased to take note of them as being anything but of the ordinary run. If a man was suspected of being involved in any breach of camp regulations, or caught out, he would be questioned with the object of finding out who else was concerned. After going through the same questions several times, and getting the same story, a blow on the mouth, either with the fist or the heel of a shoe, was the usual opening gambit. The Japanese are themselves such out and out liars that they cannot believe that anyone speaks the truth willingly: therefore (according to their trend of thought), the first story must be a pack of lies, and the truth must be extracted by third degree methods. If, by the time they had tired themselves out, the story remained unshaken, they would usually decide it was true. By these methods, of course, they did break down many men's resistance, and frequently having caught one man out, they would suddenly descend on all the rest who had been in a 'racket' with him, having elicited their names from the man they had caught.

In many cases, too, men were beaten up for small offences, and I discovered the Japanese line of thought on this. In Japan, when a child is born, a 'history sheet' is started, which is held by the police. Everything is entered up on this sheet. If, for example, the individual should help at putting out a fire, a great credit is entered on his record; if he should be summonsed or fined for parking a car in the wrong place, a debit is recorded. All such entries are in red ink, and the Japanese regard it as a terrible thing to have a red entry. Furthermore, no man or woman can obtain employment without a scrutiny of his history sheet, and a red entry is a serious bar to getting a job. So the Japanese think it is kinder to a man to deal with him summarily on the spot, by beating him up, than to cause one of the dreaded red entries to be made on his record – and they applied their own system to us.

In his diary, Peaty described prisoners being placed in detention in this way:

28 October 1943: Five men who have been in the guard-house, unsentenced, since 9 July 1943 and 13 July 1943, were released today. During this time they have not been allowed to wash or bath, shave or have their hair cut. 140 days without trial. Three of them are Johnson, Hartman, and Hilton, all Americans.

31 October 1943: Pte. Rimmer, 2nd Bn. Loyal Regt., was caught buying apples at M.K.K. two days ago. Today, he was beaten up and flung into the guard-house without being sentenced. I cannot take any steps until Monday, owing to the absence of all Japanese officers.

1 November 1943: On raising my protest about being beaten up and put in the guard-house, Pte. Rimmer was tried and given 10 days detention.

16 November 1943: Pte. Harriss and four Americans put in the guard-house for getting drunk at M.K.K. Their jackets and coats

have been taken away from them, and they have no blankets. The thermometer has been below zero degrees centigrade all day.

18 November 1943: –17C by night and –9C by day. Pte. Harriss and the others sentenced to 5 days detention for stealing alcohol.

24 July 1944: L/Sjt. Farrant, R.E. was beaten up and put in the guard-house for having Y1.35 in his pocket while going to the factory. He was subsequently given 5 days on the Probation Detail.

The prisoners routinely gave special nicknames to the guards who treated them in so many vile ways, not only to vent their own angers but to give warnings to the fellow prisoners and save them from falling into the hands of these brutes on some criminal charges. One of the guards was secretly given the name 'Evil Wolf'. This guard would beat a prisoner for not saluting quickly enough; just how quickly was quickly enough was entirely at the guard's whim.

The most notorious guard in the camp was known as 'the Bull'. His real name was Ishikawa. Nearly every POW tasted his violence.

John F Zenda (Mukden POW #424) observed that brutality by the Japanese guards was utterly commonplace. Once, just as Zenda was getting out of bed for roll call, the Bull came in screaming at him and raining blows on him. "To this day I have no idea why he was hitting me," said Zenda.

Major Peaty wrote in his diary of many cases of the Bull's violence.

8 July 1943: This morning I witnessed another of the disgusting exhibitions which are daily becoming more frequent. Pte. Rimmer, 2nd Bn. the Loyal Regt. was dealt three straight rights to the jaw, thrown to the ground and kicked by the Adjutant, Ishikawa Tai,

because he bowed while carrying a coal-scuttle and shovel, instead of putting them down. Three men were also beaten up by Miki Chui with a heavy piece of wood about three feet long, two of them being knocked right out, for having hung their blankets out to air on the rope around the barracks. A protest brought the reply that "from now on rough stuff is to be the policy". (The men were all Americans).

12 October 1943: Today has been one of beatings again: four of the American orderlies were beaten up (all knocked out with a wooden sword), for the reason that the basins in the American officers' quarters were said to be dirty. No. 954 (name unknown) received over 30 blows from the flat of Ishikawa Tai's sword. Captain Horner witnessed the whole thing, and says it was revolting. The reason (for No. 954 being beaten up) was that one of the guards said something to him, which he did not understand; Ishikawa was using his sword with both hands, and jumping clean off the ground to add force to his blows. The man had to receive medical attention.

26 October 1943: Last night, Ishikawa Tai caught five men going to the latrines with lighted cigarettes in their hands, so this morning, after keeping us waiting for nearly forty minutes on roll-call, he called them out and knocked them down, and then lunged at them with his sword (in its scabbard) and then went along the line and knocked them all down again. They were all Americans.

Ishikawa followed up his performance this morning by attacking Lieut. Levy (U.S. Signals) with his sword, for some unknown reason. Those Japanese who do not seem to be drug-addicts seem to be mad: how little the people of Europe realize what a menace they are.

Two more instances of beating up today. An elderly man, about 50, had worn out his trousers, issued nearly a year ago, and had taken them three times to the tailors shop for repair, where the Nip in charge had refused them. Lt. Miki and Murata had his trousers taken off, and beat him up pretty badly.

The other case was that of a man working on the coal-pile, who got a piece of grit in his eye. The Nip in charge refused him any chance to get it out, and took him to Miki. He was made to adopt the "press-up" position, and every time his arms gave out through fatigue, Miki, Murata and a stooge beat him unmercifully. This continued for well over half-an-hour.

11 February 1945: We bid farewell to the Bull – Ishikawa. (The Adjutant: his name translated is ISHI – stone, KAWA – river, but to everyone he was known simply as "the Bull", on account of his mad rages and complete lack of self-control.)

Of all the punishments meted out, the most terrifying one was solitary confinement.

The prisoners called it "a hell darker than the hell we all occupied". For a prisoner placed in solitary confinement, whether in the freezing dampness of winter or the boiling heat of summer, the minimum sentence was three days. Just surviving and emerging alive was the greatest of all good fortunes.

Robert Rosendahl remembered the time that he was thrown into solitary confinement for no apparent reason. The Japanese suspected him of destroying things in the camp. After two days in this solitary confinement, Rosendahl told himself to keep moving in order to stay warm, and not to sleep; if he fell asleep, he would freeze to death.

James Bollich was placed in solitary for three weeks for some unknown reason; some inadvertent offence. One morning, when Bollich and the other prisoners arrived at the plant for labour, he noticed a group of Japanese guards on the factory grounds, seemingly hiding and then coming out in the open, over the factory yard, looking very grave. In front of them, another group of guards seemed to be doing the same thing. This was actually some form of drill, but Bollich and his comrades knew nothing about Japanese soldiering, so they walked directly through the middle of the troops in order to get to their work stations in the plant. As they were setting up the machines at their work stations, a Japanese officer frantically burst in, planted himself in front of them, and began screaming. The prisoners did not understand a word he was saying, but it was obvious that the prisoners' incomprehension of what the soldiers had been doing in their drill had offended the officer. The officer gave the men a dressing down and left. After they shut the door of their work area, the men had a good laugh, not realising that the sound of their laughter was reaching the ears of the Japanese officer outside. In he came again. This time, he was in a fury. He lined the men up and slapped each of them in the face with his fan. Because Bollich was at the end of the line, he managed to slip away. But he still could not avoid disaster.

When they returned to the camp, Bollich and eight other prisoners were detained to one side. After the other men had been searched and returned to their barracks, the Japanese officer of the day and an interpreter began interrogating Bollich and the other eight prisoners. When they got to Bollich, the officer asked: "Does a Japanese officer have the right to strike a prisoner inside the factory?" Bollich replied: "I don't know." That answer did not satisfy the officer, who put the question to Bollich again. Bollich hesitated for a moment and then said again: "I don't know." That got him into big trouble. On the spot, the Japanese interpreter hit him and then threw him into solitary confinement.

After the move to the new camp, with the MKK plant less than a kilometre away, the Japanese created a barbed-wire passage especially for the prisoners to walk through on their way to and from work, so that they could have absolutely no contact with anyone on the outside. But it still gave some prisoners a chance to take a risk and try their luck.

The American POW Smith Merrill recalled that, on Christmas Eve, he and his comrades were working in the plant. One of his buddies had the idea of sneaking some alcohol that the factory used as antifreeze back to the barracks. He figured that there was no way the Japanese would conduct their usual body searches at the camp on Christmas Eve. He was utterly mistaken. At the line-up for body searches, he hid the bags of alcohol in his clothing. He saw that the Japanese were conducting their minute body searches with their usual thoroughness. When the Japanese guards were not looking, he quickly tossed the bag into a ditch behind him. Unfortunately, the Japanese discovered the two bags within an hour.

Ishikawa 'the Bull' was the officer of the day on this occasion. He assembled all the men who had worked in the plant that day on the camp exercise ground. He ordered them to stand motionless in the −20C cold, to contemplate their bad conduct. The one who had committed the offence offered to step forwards, confess and take the punishment, but his buddies did not agree and told him to keep his mouth shut. They preferred to die of cold rather than hand over one of their own. That was how the men spent Christmas Eve, standing in the bitter cold. After 12 hours, the officer arriving to replace Ishikawa ordered the men released, and the men dragged their frozen bodies back to their barracks.

The American POW Roy Weaver recounted a time when he did not hear the Bull and failed to obey the officer's order. The Bull beat him savagely with the scabbard of his sword. As Weaver put it, the Bull's brutality derived from his personal nature, but it also reflected the Japanese military idea that those who surrendered were subhuman.

Until that point, the POWs often secretly brought things out of the plant and back to the camp. After these incidents of brutality, almost none of the men dared take anything away. The men at the plant and their buddies back at the camp worked out a secret way of signalling whether the Bull was on duty or not. If the Bull was on duty, the men in the barracks would hoist a white towel from the barracks window facing the factory. When the men in the plant saw the signal, they whispered to each other: "Careful! The Bull!"

# 10

# A SECRET CONTEST

ALTHOUGH THEY LIVED a constricted existence far from the fire and smoke of the war's battlefields, the POWs still carried out their own war against the Japanese. They looked for every possible way to be secretly destructive and to carry out 'resistance war' in their own ways. When they realised that they were producing all sorts of military items, from aircraft parts to rifle components – all to be used in killing their own countrymen – it was the last straw, and the prisoners decided to fight back.

The British prisoner Arthur Christie said: "Although we are far from the battlefield and living a hard life, each of us still fights the Japanese." But the prisoners knew well that if their resistance went to extremes, the Japanese could wreak brutal punishments on them. They had already learned that lesson many times. Fortunately, they discovered that working in the plant offered many opportunities to strike back.

Oliver Allen said: "Though we had surrendered, and there were no guns in our hands, we still wanted to fight in our hearts. We tried every means to destroy things as we worked." In the early days of their labour at the factory, Allen and some of his comrades were ordered to remove a great many stones from inside the building. They loaded the rocks onto small rail carts and pushed the carts outside. There were two such carts. The men were divided into two groups, one per cart. At one point, the track went through some curves. Allen took note. He recalled: "The car came to the corner, and the prisoners deliberately accelerated the cart down the track. As a result, all the stones were turned over. One track could only transport one car at a time. The Japanese urged another group of prisoners to help, but they always found various reasons to evade. Repeatedly, the stone was unloaded, the car was returned to the track, the stone was loaded onto the car, and the car was pushed away. All morning, we kept reloading the fallen stone back into the car. As a result, only one job was done in the morning. In the afternoon, the same thing happened to another group of prisoners."

Only five hundred metres east of the new camp lay a hoist factory, a unit of TKK, where some of the POWs worked. The top of the hoists was made of a kind of hard rubber. The POWs used this and various bits of wood and metal to make simple smoking pipes. They polished and decorated them until they looked nice, and then presented them as gifts, or sold them to Japanese officers in the camp. Cigarettes were in extremely short supply at the camp, and these pipes came in very handy. Allen said: "I still have three of those pipes, and I made one of them myself." The POWs made small toys and other items for their own amusement out of the bits and pieces they pilfered from the factory.

In reality, the challenge that the POWs faced in their endless months of repression, boredom and depression, was how to find their own personal peace and meaning in their lives.

Allen said that the men passed their days gambling at cards: "We all soon became gamblers. But this was a way of staying sane. If I had just sat on my bunk, I would think about how desperate I was to go home. Sometimes I would win, sometimes I would lose, but that was also a kind of happiness. We gambled the four yen we received each month."

Allen recounted that while he was in the camp, many men were in low spirits. One of the men would tell jokes to groups of the prisoners. He had a good voice and sang well; people would ask him to sing this or that number. He was a great morale booster, and after the war he was decorated for his service.

Robert Rosendahl was one of the prisoners whose morale sank, and he had a hard time getting out of himself. While in the camp, he had no idea how things would end. He was utterly mentally unprepared. "I didn't think they would kill us," he said. "I just thought they would take us to a prison somewhere, perhaps for an exchange."

So Rosendahl kept to himself, avoiding crowds and saying little. "That was the only way I could survive. If you try to avoid it, maybe no one will make trouble for you," he said. But sometimes trouble found him anyway. He would feel especially discouraged after a beating. "In the military, we had never had any instruction about how to face the Japanese, and we were not educated how to be prisoners of war. We were all innocent lambs."

Careful and withdrawn as he was, Rosendahl was still sent to solitary confinement for no clear reason. "We were often beaten by the Japanese soldiers," he said. "They would slap your face and knock you to the ground. They liked to make you feel small." At that time, Rosendahl had been working at the MKK plant for a week when he was dismissed from his job. He was thrown into solitary confinement for a week.

For the prisoners, the contest with the Japanese sometimes became a game of wits. In their work of assembling machinery at the order of the Japanese, these American, British and Dutch prisoners of war gave the Japanese plenty of trouble.

MKK had 89 pieces of equipment of the latest American design. Before installing them, the men first had to dig trenches and pour cement footings. A group of fifty prisoners set to work, under the watchful eye of Japanese guards. When the weather was cold, at about 10am, the Japanese gathered at the corner of the factory to make a fire. Rosendahl said that, at those times, the POWs worked especially vigorously. When the guards went to make their tea, the workers would lift a new machine, deposit it in its trench and pour the cement to form the footing. By the time the Japanese returned, there were only 88 machines.

When the 88 machines were fully installed, they still would not run, because the prisoners had thrown various parts and components into the trench before they filled it with cement. The POWs opened a series of large crates, took the machine parts on the top of the contents of the boxes, and tossed them into the curing cement. This led Tokyo to send out a special investigator. When he discovered what had happened, he cried: "This is an unprecedented act of sabotage!"

Rosendahl recounted: "The Japanese didn't have any evidence at all. They didn't even know that we had thrown the things inside. I was told that my attitude was not good, so they wouldn't let me work in the factory." Subsequently, Rosendahl was given a work assignment inside the camp itself, doing odd jobs like maintaining the sewing machines and repairing shoes. The Japanese would not let him enter the factory.

POW Russell Grokett was a machine operator at MKK. On one occasion, the Japanese handed him two blueprints and told him to produce parts accordingly. Looking at the blueprints, Grokett realised that the parts were gears to be used in Japanese fighter planes. He could not abide the idea that parts he produced would be used to wage war on his own country. So he decided on his own dangerous act of sabotage: he threw one of the blueprints into the stove. The work order called for production of 64 sets of gears, half facing right and half facing left. What he produced was 64 sets of gears, all facing right. All the gears had to be discarded. The

Japanese said nothing because they themselves had forgotten whether they had given Grokett one blueprint or two.

Some POWs were eager to work in the factory rather than stay in the camp. In the factory, they could get away from the brutality of the Japanese guards for a while and escape from the camp's oppressive atmosphere. They could also encounter some Chinese people in the plant, and, when opportunities arose, they would destroy something. The Japanese foolishly thought that they could give the prisoners some parts with instructions, and they would be honestly assembled.

On one occasion, some POWs were sent to install a lathe. The top part of the machine moved back and forth and weighed several tons. The lower part was a solid footing, to which the upper part was to be fastened. The POWs pretended they were installing the machine, but when it was turned on, the base was not level. The machine ran very badly.

Sometimes a set of gears in one of the machines would mysteriously go missing. The Japanese would have to seek out the American designers of the machines to get a replica of the missing gears. That would take a month or more.

MKK produced machines for cutting soft metals. Metal blocks were inserted at one end, and the cutting machine produced the necessary number of smaller parts at the other end. This machine was an imitation of a machine produced by the American company Warner and Swasey. At the time, the machine was state of the art. The Japanese wanted to show that they were the best, so they invited some generals and important officials to come and see it. When they turned the machine on, it suddenly burst into thick smoke. The Japanese shut the machine down, put it onto a trailer and towed it away.

The Manchuria Boot Corporation was a factory producing leather footwear for the Japanese army. The POWs understandably did not want to manufacture such boots, so they altered the production process, and the boots they produced were frail and lacked durability. The American POW Smith Merrill recalled: "When the tanning process reached the final stage, we deliberately repeated the process. This resulted in leather that was as thin as a piece of paper."

Talmage Middleton, an American POW, said that one of his comrades by the name of Larry was working in the TKK plant, producing gantry cranes. Of the twenty POWs, two worked as draftsmen, and the rest worked as welders or sheet-metal workers. In order to do their sabotage without being discovered, the POWs developed some tacit understandings. The welders would guarantee that their work was good, and their welds looked perfect. But in fact the depth of their welds was not up to the work order specifications. After the welding was done, the painting crew would do what looked like a perfect job, so that the finished product completely satisfied the Japanese. What happened when the product was used can only be imagined.

In addition to all these acts of sabotage in the secret contest with the Japanese, the highest-ranking British military officer and POW representative, Major Peaty, never missed an opportunity to violate regulations and go directly into conflict with the Japanese. He would, for example, argue righteously with the Japanese over their violations of the Geneva Convention by using prisoners to work producing goods for the use of the armed forces.

While the Japanese routinely paid little attention to all of his complaining, Peaty put every effort into being the prisoners' representative. In his diary, he described some of his protests:

1 November 1944: Having allowed things to cool down a little after my last dust-up with the Superintendent, I handed him a formal letter of protest addressed to the Commandant, against the employment of Prisoners-of-War in the manufacture of aeroplane parts, asking that they be given other work, and that

the matter may be referred to a higher authority if beyond his jurisdiction.

3 November 1944: Received a reply to my letter of protest, to the effect that Japan was not a signatory of the Hague convention, and is therefore not bound to observe any of the principles of International Law.

25 February 1945: We heard that the Prisoners-of-War at Branch Camp No. 111 were being employed in the manufacture of steel helmets, and that they have protested. Those who acted as spokesmen (including Sjt. Arnott of R.A.M.C.) were beaten up by Lieut. Hyashi, following which they were taken off the presses making helmets from blank discs, and put on the presses making the discs. Lt. Hyashi said that they were not supposed to know that the discs would be made into helmets, and therefore they could do this work with a clear conscience. What a queer mentality the Japanese have: they even cheat themselves. I made my usual protest, and received the usual reply.

1 May 1945: I took up the question of Prisoners-of-War in camp who were put on the job of removing rust from, and cleaning up what appear to be 50mm Trench Mortar Bombs. Lt. Hijikata said that any men who objected would be given other work, and would not incur any punishment, and he also stated that it was only a temporary task, and that as I had protested no more would be brought into camp.

Many similar acts of sabotage occurred at all of the prisoners' workplaces. Each prisoner had his anecdotes. Needless to say, because of all this 'mischief', productivity of these plants and the quality of their products was hard to guarantee, and this led the Japanese to doubt the production skills of their prisoner workers.

An MKK investigation report found that in the first half of 1944, the defect rate was 3.5% for Chinese workers, 3.7% for Japanese workers and 7.5% for POW workers. In the second half of September, the rates were 4% for Chinese workers, 3% for Japanese workers and 7% for POW workers. The POW defect rate was twice that of the Chinese and Japanese workers' rates.

The Japanese came to the conclusion that the Allied POWs had terrible efficiency and production quality rates. Later, when General Wainwright, who had been sequestered in a different part of the camp, heard these tales, he proudly spoke of how that factory had the largest number of buried pliers, wrenches and other tools in the world. He said that the POWs had risked their lives with this brave response to the Japanese.

# 11

# THE WIND CHANGES

IN 1944, the Americans abandoned the traditional tactic of contesting every island and devastating every city in favour of a new tactic called 'island hopping', which proved successful. The Americans scored victory after victory, while the Japanese met defeat after defeat. The war began to press heavily on Japan. The Japanese fought tenaciously; each American victory exacted a heavy price. To strengthen their attack on the Japanese, the Americans borrowed from their European experience in the use of aerial bombardment. They settled on a plan for the heavy bombing of the Japanese home islands.

Moreover, they included puppet-controlled Manchukuo, Japanese rear-area transportation facilities, arsenals, mines and related strategic targets in their bombing plans. The goal was to demolish Japan's ability to make war and to shatter their military ambitions.

The bombing campaign was the responsibility of the US Air Force's 20th Bombing Group, using the latest bomber, the B-29 Superfortress. The first group of B-29s arrived at the US airbase in

Calcutta in April 1944. On 24 April, B-29s crossed the Himalayas and landed at a base outside of Chengdu, in Sichuan province.

A good deal of the success of the US bombing campaign was the result of the Chinese government's construction of forward airfields capable of handling the B-29s. 'Strategic bombing' not only targeted military objectives and vital facilities; even more importantly, it attacked civilians "with no distinction". It aimed not only to destroy the enemy's ability to wage war; it also sought to break the enemy government's and population's will to fight. In the history of global warfare, formally speaking, strategic bombing began in the Chinese theatre of war, with Japan's sustained bombing attacks on Chongqing, Chengdu, Kunming and other important urban targets in 1938.

Blood for blood, a tooth for a tooth. The US strategic bombing operation against Japan was called Operation Matterhorn. To ensure the success of Matterhorn, the Chinese government decided to carry out a 'Special Construction Plan' for the large-scale construction of airfields, using more than half a million labourers from a total of 29 locations including Chengdu, Huayang, Wenjiang, Pixian, Chongqing, Xinjin, Shuangliu, Xindu, Qionglai, Pujiang and Dayi. Four bomber airfields and five pursuit plane airfields were built in the Chengdu area. Construction began on 1 April 1944 on the bomber bases at Xinjin, Qionglai, Pengshan and Guanghan. By May, four bases for heavy aircraft, plus the associated hangars, fuel and bomb storage facilities, ammunition dumps, radio communications stations, air traffic control stations, command buildings and accommodations for troops were completed on schedule.

On 15 June 1944, 73 B-29s took off from the several airfields outside of Chengdu in Operation Matterhorn's first bombing mission against Japan. By the end of 1944, the B-29s had dropped 3,623 tons of ordnance on the Japanese home islands and Japanese-occupied territories. The Allied strategic bombing campaign against

Japan continued until the end of the war, heavily damaging Japan's military capabilities and its war spirit. The first step in the strategic bombing campaign was taken in Chengdu. That represented an important Chinese contribution to the anti-Fascist war effort.

In Manchukuo, the main US strategic bombing targets were Japanese-controlled mines and arsenals, as well as railroads, ports and related transportation hubs. They included the Showa Steel Works in Anshan, the Mukden Arsenal, the Manchuria Aircraft Factory and the Benxi Steel Mill in Benxi.

Some of these targets were struck repeatedly.

Showa Steel suffered large-scale attacks on 29 July, 8 September and 26 September, with various degrees of damage. In the 29 July raid, Showa Steel was hit by 95 bombs, heavily damaging the coking plant and sintering mill. A hundred people died in that raid, and another 170 were injured. Production capacity dropped by 300,000 tons. The Japanese estimated that repairs would take at least one month.

As the winter of 1944 began, air-raid alarms sounded constantly in Japanese-occupied Mukden. The common Chinese people there, who had suffered the loss of their own country, lived in constant terror. To confuse the American bombers, the Japanese regularly set fires to form smoke screens. On 7 December 1944, the third anniversary of the Pearl Harbor attack, the US 20th Bombing Group sent 108 B-29s from Chengdu to hit targets in Mukden. Japanese radar picked up the bombers before they reached Mukden, and the Japanese lit smokescreens at many points in the city, around vital military targets such as weapons plants and ammunition dumps. Walt E Huss (Mukden POW #1887), who participated in this raid, recalled that the Japanese smokescreen tactic only gave the US high-altitude bomb crews a clearer sense of where their targets were.

Loudspeaker announcers shouted themselves hoarse warning of the approach of the American planes. The wail of air-raid sirens filled the city. Japanese air bases around the edges of the city stood ready to launch their planes against the American bombers. At about 10am, the vast fleet of American planes appeared on the southwestern horizon. According to plan, 80 B-29s struck the Mukden Arsenal and the Manchuria Aircraft Factory. Another ten planes targeted a rail yard, while several more bombed the railway station and some temporary cargo yards.

Japanese anti-aircraft was ineffective against the B-29s, which flew at high altitude. According to some elderly residents of Mukden who experienced the raid that day, the ground-based Japanese guns did not hit the B-29s, their shells exploding harmlessly with puffs of smoke below the bombers and posing no threat to them. In fact, once the Americans embarked upon the strategic bombing campaign, neither the Japanese ground-based anti-aircraft weaponry nor their fighter planes were of any use. We could say that the B-29s entered a realm where no men intruded, and could pretty much bomb where they liked. On 20 August, a fleet of 72 B-29s from Chengdu, attacking Yawata in northern Kyūshū, for the first time ran into suicide attacks by Japanese fighter planes. Fourteen B-29s were attacked, and eight were brought down. After that, suicide attacks became Japan's secret weapon against the B-29s, and the Japanese military began organising aerial suicide squads.

On 7 December, the Japanese put 50 fighter planes into the air from airfields around Mukden when the air-raid alarms sounded. The fighters carried out fierce suicide attacks on the bombers. The agile Japanese fighters swarmed the bomber formations, and although the bombers were heavily armed, seven B-29s were shot down by the Japanese that day. The B-29s crashed at Yongle village in the Sujiatun district of Mukden, Yonganqiao in Yuhong district, Yang Shibao village in Yuhong district, and two locations in Tai'an county of Anshan. To brag about their military success, the

Japanese mounted the remains of one of the engines of a fallen B-29 in a park in the city of Mukden.

According to official records, B-29 number 42-6390, nicknamed Gallopin' Goose, was the first Superfortress brought down by the Japanese over Mukden. The plane's tail gunner, Arnold G Pope (Mukden POW #1884), was the only survivor of the plane's eleven-man crew. He parachuted from the plane and was captured by Japanese forces; the other ten men lost their lives at Mukden. B-29 number 42-24486, known as Windy City II, was flying close to Gallopin' Goose when the latter was hit. Staff Sergeant William Wootten described the scene: "The fighter came in at us low and I gave him 50 rounds when he was 400 yards away. The fighter's right engine started smoking and burning." Wootten saw pieces of the canopy fly off. Going down out of control and smoking profusely, the fighter then pulled up and slipped under Gallopin' Goose, hitting the left horizontal and vertical stabiliser and tearing them off. "I saw one parachute come out of 42-6390 before it hit the ground," said Wootten.

B-29 number 42-6299, known as Humpin' Honey, collided with a Japanese fighter and crashed in a field outside the city. Two men opened their parachutes, but another two, shot and unconscious, failed to open theirs. The remainder of the crew lost their lives in the crash. The bomber burned fiercely, and, except for a few bones, no recognisable remains could be found.

On 21 December, an unnamed B-29 took off with its group from Chengdu. Crossing the Bohai Gulf, it entered Japanese airspace at Mukden. Approaching the city before making its bomb run, the plane was struck by a Japanese fighter and spun out of control. It began to disintegrate and went into a vertical dive. The bomber crashed into a frozen pond at Yangshitun in Mukden. The fuselage burst into flames, and its bomb load exploded one after another. Yangshitun was littered with pieces of the plane and chunks of ice thrown up by the exploding bombs, falling like raindrops from the sky. A number of houses and many windows were blown apart. Falling debris punched holes in a number of roofs. But happily, as the plane fell to earth, it missed the village, and no local residents were killed or wounded. The Japanese fighter plane that collided with the B-29 crashed and burned in the nearby village of Yuliangcun, and its pilot died.

Of the eleven crewmen on the Old Campaigner, only one man, Elbert L Edwards (Mukden POW #1885), who had been shot, managed to get out of the plane. All the others died in the inferno; no complete remains could be found. After the war, along with fragments of the plane, some human remains were excavated at the scene of the crash. The remains were placed into three caskets and transported back to the US for burial in Arlington National Cemetery. Because the battle had taken place at high altitude, where the air was thin, Edwards lost consciousness after he bailed out. Luckily, his parachute opened, and he landed in an open field about one and a half kilometres from his plane.

Edwards recounted that shortly after landing he regained consciousness. Japanese soldiers rushed up and surrounded him. One of the Japanese tried to take the ring from his finger but he recoiled. The soldier raised his dagger as if to cut off Edwards' finger, and the airman had no choice but to relinquish his cherished high school graduation ring. Then the Japanese blindfolded him and tied his hands behind his back, threw him into a truck and drove him to a prison. In March 1945, Edwards was transferred to the Mukden POW camp, to be liberated with his fellow POWs only after the Japanese surrender.

B-29 number 42-6359, known as Missouri Queen, belonging to the 462nd Bomb Group, took part in the mission on 7 December. After dropping its bombs, the plane was headed back to base, when First Lieutenant Johnson radioed that he did not have enough fuel to get back and would have to look for a friendly airfield where he could fill his tanks. That was the last anyone heard from Missouri

Queen. The plane was reported down in the Qinyuan mountains of Shanxi province. No trace of the eleven-man crew, including Lieutenant Johnson, has ever been found, and the men are to this day listed as missing in action.

On 7 December, the target for B-29 number 42-6389, known as Party Girl, was the Manchuria Aircraft Manufacturing Plant. The bomber loosed its bombs smoothly and had turned towards home, when the squadron leader radioed the pilot of the Party Girl, Lieutenant Calvin L Lyons, to drop to a lower altitude to disappear into the cloud bank looming in front of them. Entering the cloud bank at this lower altitude, Lyons noticed that his wings were icing, and decided to climb out of the clouds. But by then Party Girl had lost contact with its squadron. Although the base radioed for more than an hour, there was no response from Party Girl. Finally, it crashed, and all eleven on board were killed.

B-29 number 42-6262, known as Round Trip Ticket, crashed after its bomb run in a coastal area of western Liaoning. The crew of eleven were killed. The Japanese removed the remains from the plane and discarded them at an unknown location. After some Chinese farmers found the discarded remains, they dug a mass grave and buried them, so that they could be recovered after the war.

In the two bombing raids of 7 and 21 December, nine American B-29s were lost, and 85 crewmen died. Another 14 were captured. The brave American officers and crewmen contributed their blood and their youth at Mukden.

Two of the men on Old Campaigner were new fathers: Captain Benedict and Lieutenant Dailey. Their daughters were born while they were serving courageously on the battlefield. Neither would ever see his daughter. Later, their comrade, Elbert Edwards, the only survivor from Old Campaigner, named his own two children after the daughters of his lost crewmates, in order to remember their sacrifice. From the bomber's crew of eleven, only those four descendants remained.

Charles Krueger, first lieutenant on the Humpin' Honey, died in the 7 December raid. Not long after he went overseas to fight, his twin sons were born. The boys never saw their father. His widow lived to an old age. In my email interviews with her in 2006, she told me that she hoped to come to Shenyang to see the place where her husband had perished.

# 12

# BLOODY MUKDEN

As THE WAR SITUATION WORSENED, the Japanese army issued a document regarding the treatment of prisoners of war under crisis conditions. The vice minister of the army sent Land Forces Asia Secret Order Number 1633 to all relevant units on 1 September 1944. The order read:

In accordance with the changing war situation, prisoners of war shall be dealt with according to the following plan:

1. To prevent POWs and those detained by our forces from falling into the hands of the enemy, specific locations must be chosen for facilities designated for the concentration of POWs and arrestees along with specific plans for moving them.

2. Under enemy attack, as a last resort, such POWs and detainees may be released.

3. According to Article 6 of the Regulations on Handling of Prisoners of War, as a last resort and for purposes of self-defence,

extraordinary measures may be taken, but actions that will further stimulate the enemy's hatred or a pretext for the enemy's propaganda are to be avoided.

Recipients of this order included the Southern Command, China Expeditionary Forces Headquarters and the Japanese Garrison Headquarters in Taiwan and Hong Kong. What were the so-called "extraordinary measures" mentioned in the order? We do not know for sure, but if we consider what we know about the Japanese military, the situation of the Allied POWs was sure to get more difficult and more complex once the American bombing began.

The bombing attacks of 7 December 1944 caused heavy damage to many Japanese installations and military targets in Mukden. The losses were especially heavy at the Mukden Arsenal and the Manchuria Aircraft Manufacturing Plant. The former was almost completely demolished and unable to regain normal production throughout the remainder of the war. But the Mukden POW camp, less than a kilometre north of the arsenal, also took hits. Three bombs landed inside the camp, with heavy casualties both of dead and wounded.

Major Peaty, writing on the day of the bombing and over the next few days, recorded the carnage. Through his diary, we can glimpse the military grit and strength of purpose of the Allied prisoners in the face of calamity. Their indomitable fighting spirit was the hardest obstacle for the Japanese to overcome.

7 December 1944: 9.10am Air Raid "Yellow", 9.50am Air Raid "Red" almost immediately followed by a salvo of bombs which fell close by, dealing very effectively with a small-arms ammunition factory about 1km to the north of the camp. (I believe twelve bombs hit the factory: at any rate, it never functioned again). Following this salvo, we dispersed as widely as possible and laid flat on the parade ground. A second wave of B-29s came

over, and two bombs fell in the camp, one of which hit No.2 Barracks latrine and set it afire, although it did not explode. The other, which did explode, dropped right among us on the parade ground, causing 54 casualties, 16 being killed outright. There is only one stretcher in camp, but we tore down goal-posts, etc., and carried them all there before the next wave came over. L/Bdr. Scholl, R.A. was the only one of the British killed, and Sjt. Gooby, Pte. Chapman, and Pte. Minshall, all the Loyals, were badly wounded. S/Sjt. Hanson R.A.O.C., Cpl. Clancy, A.I.F. Cpl Feeney, Loyals; Pte. Anstis, A.I.F., Ptes. Duckworth and Dickenson, Loyals, slightly injured. Immediately after the raid, and while the Japanese were still out of control, we dug slit trenches all over the parade ground, in spite of previously having been forbidden to do so. Sjt. Russell of the R.A.M.C. did excellent work in instructing those acting as stretcher bearers as to which of the casualties should be taken to hospital, and Pte. Vaughan, R.A.M.C., although stone deaf, and liable to drop at the slightest exertion, from a weak heart, went at once to the hospital and did good work. Discipline was superb.

8 December 1944: All hands still digging slit trenches, but the factory workers were sent to M.K.K. in the afternoon. We completed 1,100ft of trenching by dusk, enough to accommodate all the men in camp. The general estimate of the number of planes is 83, which came over in seven waves. I saw a Japanese fighter attack a B-29, and the pilot bale out, and soon after five parachutes left the B-29.

9 December 1944: Pte. Chapman had his leg almost severed by the bomb, and it was removed the same day. He was lucky in being one of the first taken to hospital, as he got the only shot of anti-gas gangrene serum. Pte. Minshull's left arm was amputated yesterday. It is amazing to see how cheerful they are – calling

123

each other "Wingy" and "Stumpy". It had been hoped to save Sjt. Gooby's leg, but gangrene set in, and it has been removed today. Two more men died of their wounds yesterday, making the death toll 18, and I'm afraid that Gooby has only a slim chance, as his gangrene is terrible. All electricity and water has been put out of action, and not yet restored, so we are back to using the well. The Japanese emergency lighting system consisted of five candles for the whole camp, but Dr. Brennan has managed to conceal a packet he brought from Singapore right up to now, and with the aid of these the doctors operated on the wounded up to 1am on the night of the bombing, when they had to give up as the candles had all been consumed. As all the windows were blown out, we lit all the petshkas without asking permission to do so, and the Japanese got nasty about it, but we more or less ignored them.

10 December 1944: Sunday – a factory holiday, which we imployed to dig more slit trenches … Carried out a P.A.D. test, and found that there is plenty of room for everyone in the slit trenches. … L/Sjt. Gooby died at 7.15pm.

12 December 1944: I asked for Gooby's and Scholl's bodies to be covered with the Union Jack at the funeral, and for the Last Post to be blown. The latter request was granted, and the former refused.

13 December 1944: The casualties were actually 54 – 19 dead and 35 wounded. Just before noon, we received a visit from a single plane, which was fired at, but apparently it dropped nothing. The Japanese offered facilities for the making and safe custody of wills. Everyone is to be given the opportunity to send a ten-word radiogram, or with the Commandant's permission, a longer one, and the range of transmission is increased to include North and South America, Canada, Australia, New Zealand, India and Great

Britain. Today, all the wounded and the officers have been asked to write a statement about the accident which we understand will be broadcast to the U.S. Air Corps based in China.

18 December 1944: The Commandant made a speech about the bombing, in which he said that the Japanese Intelligence had proved it was all a deliberate attack on us, by the fact that the bomb that hit the building was a demolition bomb, and the one that fell in the parade ground was an anti-personnel bomb. He did not attempt to explain why it was that if they could place these two so nicely, they should have been so careless as to let most of the others hit an ammunition factory.

When I interviewed him, Robert Rosendahl couldn't remember whether he had gone to his labour at MKK that morning. "The bomber appeared on the horizon, flew straight over the camp and began bombing," he said. "The prisoners all dispersed on the ground because there were no bunkers. A total of three bombs hit the prison camp. One bomb fell on the toilet block on the west side of the barracks, but it did not explode. When we went to the toilet, there was golden fire on the water."

Rosendahl added: "The bombing killed many people. I can't remember how many. Some people lost their arms, some lost their legs, some were hit. Many people were injured." Rosendahl and other prisoners ran to where the Japanese stored their shovels and spades, and then to the yard, where they dug pits frantically in hopes of finding shelter the next time the bombs fell. "The Americans lost a plane during the bombing," he said. "The Japanese fired a direct hit. The plane exploded immediately, and the shells exploded together with the plane. The thing I remember the most is seeing the plane exploding, the four engines descending from the sky with heavy smoke. There were no parachutes. All of the people on the plane died during the explosion."

After the war, at a golf course in St Louis, Missouri, Rosendahl was paired with a man who had flown in a B-29 on the Mukden bomb run that day. They talked about the losses in the camp. The flyer said: "We weren't bombing you. Maps showed that as an assembly and storage facility for the Manchuria Aircraft plant. But the bomb bay doors on one of our planes jammed, and some bombs were stuck inside. One of our crew climbed down into the bomb bay and kicked the bombs loose with his feet. Those must have been the bombs that landed in the POW camp."

Oliver Allen recounted: "I remember there must have been a hundred planes flying in formation. A hundred planes simultaneously emitting the same roar overhead. It was shocking, and the Japanese were shaken by it. The Japanese aircraft factory was burning badly and took heavy losses. There was a special workshop where the Japanese were manufacturing an aircraft. They ordered the prisoners to work on it, but some of the prisoners refused."

The POWs who had refused to work on the plane were sent back to the camp and confined. Allen said he completely understood their refusal: "They knew that we were making planes that would be used to slaughter our fathers, our brothers, our sisters."

The prisoners in the Mukden POW camp not only underwent a baptism of fire; they went through a life-and-death test under the brutal treatment of the Japanese. This sudden bombing, which seemed to come from nowhere, brought pain and suffering, but also the whiff of hope gradually coming into play. Despite their losses from this bombing, the prisoners' morale never wavered. In fact, it only grew stronger, as a feeling of optimism and upward advance set in.

Oliver Allen saw a fellow prisoner lose his right arm during the bombing and tried to comfort him. But not only did the wounded man not complain; he said to Allen: "Never mind – I'm left-handed!"

When the bombs suddenly landed, many of the prisoners panicked, running in every direction, looking for places to hide. Some, however, remained calm. Some of the men threw themselves on the ground, lying on their backs. One of them gave his comrades a running commentary about the number of planes in the sky and the squadrons they belonged to, oblivious to the danger to himself. He had probably been a flyer himself before being captured; he seemed to be flying in blue skies once again. Allen said: "The Japanese didn't enjoy our B-29 bombing, but we yelled, 'You're welcome here! Blow it up!'"

On 21 December 1944, bombers from the Twentieth Bomb Group took off again from Chengdu to hit Mukden. This time, the bombers had no effect on the Mukden camp. Major Peaty recorded in his diary:

21 December 1944: Preliminary air-raid warning at 10am. Very wisely, the factory workers were brought back at once, for at 10.20 the "Red" went, and at 10.30 planes were overhead. Four waves came over, 10, 9, 10 and 10 each, and the All-clear sounded at noon. I saw one of the bombers explode in mid-air – a marvellous spectacle – and others saw Jap fighters in trouble. Nothing was dropped close enough to worry us, especially as we were all in the slit trenches before the actual alarm, but judging by the sounds, the raid fulfilled its purpose.

The Japanese forces tried to block the bombings of 7 and 21 December, but with their ground-based anti-aircraft defences ineffective, they turned to suicide tactics, sacrificing themselves to bring down the enemy. They brought down six B-29s, and three more bombers crashed for unknown reasons. Fourteen flyers parachuted safely, but the remaining 85 crew members sacrificed their young lives.

The fate of those 85 men was unknown because the Japanese would not reveal whether or not they had been taken prisoner.

The Japanese reasoning was this: only men captured in direct battle were genuine prisoners of war. Because the strategic bombing campaign targeted civilian populations far from the battlefront, the captured bomber crews were no different from the bomber crews in the air and were to be treated as war criminals. They made the captured crew sign a statement acknowledging that their actions were indistinguishable from the bombing of civilians. Thus they refused to concede that these men were prisoners of war.

On 13 August 1942, the commander of Japan's China Expeditionary Army issued China Expeditionary Army Military Law Order Number 4: Military Law on the Handling of Enemy Aircraft Crews. For the crimes of terrorising civilian populations, destroying non-military targets and similar crimes, the law prescribed sentences of 80 years or execution by firing squad. The law was to be applied specifically in the Japanese home islands, Manchuria and all war zones occupied by the China Expeditionary Army.

Happily, the B-29 crew captured at Mukden were not executed, but neither were they confined at the Mukden POW camp as prisoners of war. Instead, they were held in a unique facility; a sealed-off courtyard about 800 metres east of the main prison camp. This arrangement was in keeping with the way that the Japanese managed themselves. The Japanese military management system established yet another form of detention instrument, mainly for the purpose of housing ordinary battlefield detainees. Such facilities existed side by side with the regular prison camps, and the heads of such facilities often became the successors to departing prison camp commandants.

Elbert Edwards, the only survivor of the crash of B-29 number

42-24715, known as Old Campaigner, recalled that just after he parachuted to the ground, Japanese soldiers rushed up to take him captive. They blindfolded him with a black cloth, tied his hands behind his back, threw him into a truck and took him to a prison. In March 1945, he and 13 other American survivors were transferred to a unique and secret facility close to the east side of the POW camp. Because the Japanese used black cloth to blindfold their captives at such moments of transition, Edwards had no idea where he was.

Even in the official records of the prison camp, the names of these captives were excluded. Related information, such as their names and ranks and the names of their units remained concealed.

The 14 captured B-29 crewmen remained in secret detention in an ordinary-looking courtyard close to the POW camp. A road running along the northern edge of the courtyard separated it from the TKK works. But the POWs working in the TKK plant knew nothing of any of this. Major Peaty recorded in his diary:

28 March 1945: Fourteen rations have been sent out of camp today, and the Japanese asked us to contribute forks and spoons for the Prisoners-of-War, who have evidently been housed nearby, as the food went out cooked. From the fact that they had nothing to eat with, I think they are probably airmen.

To verify Peaty's guess, the POWs charged with delivering food thought up a method. In the words of the captured flyer Walt Huss: "One day, those of us who were held secretly found pieces of paper in our rice, with the words, 'Who are you?' The meal was sent from the prison camp. The barrel used to hold soup had a hollow handle with paper and a pencil." From that point on, the 14 secretly detained flyers were in contact with the men in the POW camp itself.

# 13

# A GATHERING OF GENERALS

A TOTAL OF 76 GENERALS – four lieutenant generals, 23 major generals and 49 brigadier generals – were taken prisoner by the Japanese in the course of the Pacific war. Of these, 19 were American, 41 were British, four were Australian, and 12 were Dutch. As the fortunes of war shifted, these men were repeatedly moved, from Manila to Taiwan and from Taiwan to Mukden. The timing and the route of each of these transfers was a result of shifts in conditions on the battlefields.

Early in the war, the Japanese military displayed insufferable arrogance. After their surprise naval and air attacks on US and British bases in the Pacific and Southeast Asia, they seized control of the seas and the skies, while continuing to advance and overcome resistance in both areas. These successive victories, however, were only temporary. When the US, which had for so long stayed on the sidelines, entered the war, it was a certainty that the Japanese had brought an invincible foe down upon themselves.

A conflict on the scale of the Pacific war was fundamentally a test of national power. Economically speaking, the gap between the power of the United States and the power of Japan was simply too huge. Steel production in Japan was a twentieth of America's. Japanese aircraft production capacity was a tenth of that of the US. Even Japan's shipbuilding capabilities, in which the Japanese took such pride, was only a third of the Americans' capacity. In 1942, as the US shifted to a war economy at Roosevelt's demand, it produced 45,000 aeroplanes, 45,000 tanks and eight million tons of shipping. A glance at numbers like this makes clear that the defeat of Japan was simply a matter of time.

Nevertheless, the Japanese held prisoner several dozen Allied general officers, who made for a considerable supply of bargaining chips. General Wainwright, for example, was the highest-ranking officer ever taken prisoner in the history of the American military. The Japanese considered Wainwright to be their 'secret treasure' from the Greater East Asia War. They published the notes of Wainwright and other officers in 1944 under the title, 'The Greater East Asia War – Prisoners' Notes', and used it to propagandise about Japan's 'Illustrious Wartime Military Achievements'.

In the latter half of 1942, the war situation underwent a major change, as the Pacific war entered its second phase. Japan's advance ran into serious obstacles, while Allied forces, starting to resist with greater strength, gained early victories. At about 3am on 11 August, the Japanese suddenly carried out a transfer of all the military officers held prisoner at the Tarlac prison camp in northern Luzon, moving the prisoners out of the Philippines entirely. On 14 August, the Tarlac prisoners arrived in the port of Kaohsiung, Taiwan. The next day they boarded the Kotani Maru, reaching the prison camp at Hualien on 16 August. Because an American general was among the prisoners, the Japanese declared a holiday and ordered all residents of the city to line the streets for a look at a captured US general.

In actual fact, all this moving of general-rank prisoners was directly related to changes in the military situation. In the first place, at the Battle of Midway in early June, American naval and air forces sank four heavy Japanese aircraft carriers and a heavy cruiser, and destroyed 250 Japanese planes; the Americans lost a single heavy carrier, one destroyer and 150 aircraft. It was the Americans' first victory since the outbreak of the Pacific war, the tip of the blade slicing into the Japanese forces. The Americans opened a bloody battle for Guadalcanal in August. Both sides threw major forces into a battle that had to be won.

This period saw three major island battles and six large naval confrontations. Japan suffered repeated maulings, losing 892 warplanes and 2,362 flyers. Those losses could never be made up.

Because they had lost control of the air, and their sea lines had been disrupted, the beleaguered Japanese military decided in mid-February 1943 to relinquish Guadalcanal. The successful American assault on Guadalcanal was a turning point in the war. The Japanese failed to regain the military initiative, and their forces were grievously weakened. In the end, having lost the military initiative, they had to turn from being the initiating force in the war to being the object of their enemy's initiative. In addition, after six months of bitter fighting around Papua in the southwest Pacific, Allied forces smashed Japan's hopes of gaining Port Moresby.

Once the American naval and air forces had fully seized the initiative, they turned from defence to attack. With the main Japanese forces decimated, a fundamental change took place in the overall Pacific war picture. As these changes developed, Japan's treatment of prisoners of war changed as well, as did Japanese treatment of its general-officer-level POWs. The cockiness with which the Japanese treated these prisoners in the early stages of the war gradually withered.

At approximately 10pm on 8 September 1942, a total of 357 high-ranking POWs held in Singapore, Hong Kong, Malaya and the Dutch East Indies were transferred to the detention camp in Hualien, Taiwan. On 27 September, five American generals and 20 officers of colonel rank were sent to the Hualien camp. At that point, the Hualien camp held all of the high-ranking military and civilian POWs. A total of 76 of these prisoners held the rank of brigadier general or higher. The number and positions of these highly-ranked prisoners were unprecedented in history.

After the outbreak of the Pacific war, Taiwan's status changed. Previously under the direct control of the Ministry of the Interior, Taiwan was declared to be the 'Second Interior', or the 'Preparatory Interior', and a process of 'Preparing for National Interior Status' was carried out. Taiwan became the base for the Japanese military's subsequent advance southward and a protective shield guarding the Japanese home islands. During the war, goods shipped to Japan from Southeast Asia had to traverse the Taiwan Strait.

Taiwan was the linchpin connecting the home territories with Japan's occupied territories in China and its supply lines from Southeast Asia. Japan used massive military forces to guard this vital maritime lifeline.

Japan moved its high-ranking POWs from Manila and the Philippines to Taiwan and did likewise with its ranking prisoners of various nationalities who had been taken in Southeast Asia. This showed Taiwan's offensive and defensive significance as Japan searched for a way of turning the trend of the war in a new direction.

The high-ranking POWs in Taiwan faced shortages of food and medicines, as well as brutal treatment at the hands of their Japanese captors. What was even more difficult for them, however, was the complete loss of respect.

For example, Japanese regulations posted in the prison camp stated whether the prisoner's rank was high or low. Any prisoner not wearing a hat was required to bow before any Japanese he encountered. Any prisoner wearing a hat was required to salute all Japanese officers and soldiers.

Whenever someone came into the camp, all prisoners were required to rise to their feet immediately and remain at attention.

The first person before whom General Wainwright had to bow was a Japanese soldier. For an American general to have to bow before a common Japanese soldier was a profound humiliation.

The first time that General Wainwright was beaten was a night in December. After roll call, at about eight in the evening, about half an hour before lights out, Wainwright picked up a towel and went to the toilet located behind his barracks. On the way, he encountered a short, sturdily built Japanese sentry. The sentry ordered him to approach, and Wainwright did.

"What are you doing?" the sentry asked. Several other American officers nearby stopped in their tracks. After only two words, the sentry slapped Wainwright full in the face. This was a heavy blow. Wainwright was furious. But as a military man, he remained standing. The sentry arrogantly struck Wainwright a second time, and a third and a fourth. At each blow, the sentry hysterically shouted: "This is for the Japanese people in the United States!" Wainwright became unsteady on his feet, but he struggled to remain standing. Seeing this, the soldier struck Wainwright on the lower left jaw, and Wainwright fell to the ground, dazed.

Semi-conscious, this was the worst humiliation he had suffered in his lifetime. He would never forget it.

The British Major General Lewis Heath had suffered a war wound in his left arm, and he routinely used a rope brace connected to the left-hand pocket of his trousers. On one occasion, he encountered a Japanese soldier, and raised his hand to salute, according to regulations. The Japanese soldier decided that the salute was too careless, and struck the general on the left arm with the butt of his rifle. Heath fell to the ground, nearly losing consciousness. Weeks after the assault, his eyes were like bloody orbs, and he still had to use a sling for his injured arm.

After the fall of Hong Kong, the British governor, Sir Mark Aitchison Young, and other senior government officials were taken prisoner by the Japanese and confined at the same facility where

General Wainwright was held. Young was a highly educated man, unaccustomed to saluting before the Japanese. The Japanese hung his sword from his neck as a threat. Young's son Brian said that when his father was taken to Taiwan, the Japanese would parade him around on the streets to humiliate him.

General Arthur Percival was captured while serving as commander of British forces in Malaya. His son recounted: "My father noted in his memoirs that after they were captured, many POWs became devoutly religious – even those who were not believers began to worship. After they entered the prison camp, religion became an important part of life and boosted their morale. I remember one time we received a letter from my father, but couldn't read it at all. The Japanese army cut a lot of the content, and the letter was full of holes."

Most of the physical abuse took place without cause. Sometimes the Japanese guards would line up twenty or thirty prisoners outside the communal toilet and would walk down the line of men, slapping each one in the face. No one could accept this treatment lightly. Everyone wanted to strike back. But the prisoners could only swallow their anger, patiently, patiently, always patiently. I visited General Wainwright's nephew, Peter Wainwright, in 2011 and 2012. He said to me: "Once, because he did not bow sufficiently to a Japanese guard, he was beaten and fell to the ground. Two US military officers witnessed the scene and wanted to rush forwards and stop the Japanese guard. But General Wainwright ordered them to step back, and he said: 'Leave me alone or he will shoot you.'"

Many officers died in the Taiwan prison camp. After a savage beating by the Japanese, the health of British Major General Merton Beckwith-Smith worsened. On 11 November 1942, he became the first high-ranking Allied officer to die while in Japanese hands.

On 2 April 1943, the Japanese once again moved their high-ranking captives. What was particular about this move was that they dispatched POWs of brigadier-general rank or higher to a camp at

Yuli, but kept those with the rank of colonel or below at Hualien. Clearly, the Japanese had other plans in mind for their captured generals; confining them in isolation ensured that they could be more easily dealt with.

On 15 June, the Japanese went a step further in reducing the size of the contingent of highest-ranking officers, transferring them to yet another camp, this one in Mucha, outside of Taipei. This small group of 14, from various countries, were the highest-ranking generals and military officers, including General Wainwright, along with a few of their attendants.

The year 1943 marked the great transition in the Pacific war. After Guadalcanal, American forces commenced their systematic large-scale counter-offensives. Further north in the Pacific, the Americans began using their 'island hopping' tactics, landing on Attu in the Aleutian Islands in May and annihilating the Japanese garrison there. The Aleutians were fully recovered by August. In the southwest Pacific and the south Pacific, American forces launched campaigns in New Guinea and the Solomon Islands in June.

They took the towns of Salamua and Lae in September and the islands of New Georgia in October. They came ashore at Bougainville in November, forcing the Japanese there to withdraw and scatter. Simultaneously, the Americans attacked the Gilbert Islands in the central Pacific and began to move westward. On 1 December, China, the UK and the US issued the Cairo Declaration pledging that all Chinese territories occupied by Japan, including Taiwan and the Pescadores which had been under Qing imperial control, would be returned to China. This was unquestionably significant, not only in military and political terms, but in terms of international law. It undoubtedly caused tremors in Japan's fierce determination to hold on to Taiwan.

In addition to dividing up their senior military prisoners, as described above, the Japanese adopted new policies regarding them. Once the ranking prisoners had been placed at Mucha, all beatings stopped. The prisoners' food improved markedly. The prisoners were no longer required to perform labour. Needless to say, the Japanese did all this for a reason. The commander of all POW camps on Taiwan made genial visits to the camp.

The Japanese finally revealed their trump card. They arranged for their officers to meet continually with individual POWs. The men would go outside the camp for picnics in the mountains or fishing excursions. They asked the individual prisoners to write letters to the heads of their respective governments, asking them to discontinue the war against Japan. If the POWs' countries would do that, the proposed letters stated, the war could come to a quick end. This abnormal initiative made crystal clear the intention to use the ranking prisoners of war as bargaining chips.

One day, a Japanese officer dashed up to Wainwright and King, saying that the International Committee of the Red Cross had sent him, and proposing to make a newsreel for broadcast in the US. General King wrote in his diary on 9 March 1944:

This morning the interpreter came to me very ashamed and apologetic and said the commandant at the head office (Col. Sazawa, I think) would like Wainwright and me to add three ideas to our dialogue for the talking pictures that are to be taken, namely:

1. That it was impossible to resist the Japanese soldiers "conviction of victory".

2. That the longer the war against the Japanese is continued, the more American soldiers will be killed.

3. That an early peace is much to be desired.

I told him I would discuss this with Wainwright, but that I was certain neither of us could say the things requested. The interpreter then asked that I give him a chit to that effect if we could not comply. He also said they would begin taking the pictures this afternoon. Wainwright of course agreed with me and I have handed the interpreter a chit signed by both of us as follows:

"Although prisoners, we are still officers of the United States Army. To make the statements that were suggested to us this morning would be inconsistent with our duty to our Government and contrary to the regulations of our army governing the conduct of officers."

After much thought, Wainwright finally accepted the demand, on condition that the content of the newsreel as proposed by the Japanese be revised. In the newsreel, the two generals appeared gaunt. They talked about life in their camp. Although their words were rigorously censored by the Japanese, the newsreel at least revealed to Americans that the two generals were alive. The same thing happened with British General Arthur Percival, as he recorded in his memoir:

At Moksak we had another example of Japanese deceit. They were very anxious for some reason to get a "talkie" film showing the supposed conditions under which we were living and our general satisfaction with them. It was probably required for propaganda purposes. They started by saying that the Red Cross required the film, but soon it became obvious that it could be nothing whatever to do with the Red Cross, for they produced a list of subjects about which people were to talk. I refused to have anything to do with it, protesting that it was against my instructions. Great pressure was brought to bear as it was obvious that they were very anxious that I should appear in the film.

Finally, a message was brought from the camp commandant to the effect that, if I refused to take part in the film, I should not be sent home when the time came for repatriation. I replied that I would be quite happy to receive that decision as the Japanese would not be in control when that happy moment arrived. The movie men duly arrived and the film was taken. The next day there was an invitation from the camp commander to go to a neighbouring river to fish. It was the first time anybody had been outside the narrow confines of the camp for six months and some accepted the invitation. When they arrived, the movie men were lined up on the bank. But there was a danger that there might be no fish, or, if there were, that they would not be caught. To provide against that eventuality, a live fish had been brought out in a can and was duly affixed to one of the rods before the photograph was taken!

With the drama of the war shifting, the Japanese were forced to create a Plan for Defence of the Homeland. The shifting war situation brought shifts in the POWs circumstances as well. This meant moving the ranking prisoners once again. This time they chose to send them to the place where the whole war of aggression had begun – Manchuria.

The 14 senior officers were transferred on 5 October 1944. Aeroplanes first took them from Taiwan to Kyūshū. From there, they were taken by train to Beppu, where they met other captured generals who had arrived four days earlier.

The men had not seen each other since they had been separated at the Yuli camp in June 1943. After two days, the prisoners moved again, by ship to Busan, Korea. From Busan, they were taken north by train to the Manchurian border. They arrived at the Zhengjiatun POW camp, located at present-day Shuangliao city in the province of Jilin, on 14 October 1944. This camp was the 'Number One Branch Camp of the Mukden POW Camp'. With that, 72 officers holding the rank of general were detained there (three of the original 76 had died, and one Dutch officer had been sent to Sumatra). Also transferred to this site were 476 captured colonels. Two years after their imprisonment at Hualien, they gathered once more in Japanese-controlled Manchuria.

On 1 December 1944, 16 senior officers were again selected from the larger group and transferred to another camp in Japanese-held Manchuria. This was in Xi'an county, located at present-day Liaoyuan in Jilin province. It was known as 'Number Two Branch Camp of the Mukden POW Camp', the local Northern Big Camp run by the Kwantung Army Liaoyuan Guards. From the time of his surrender in the Philippines on 9 June 1942, General Wainwright had been held at six POW facilities: Tarlac in the Philippines; Hualien, Yuli and Mucha in Taiwan; Zhengjiatun and now the camp in Xi'an county in Manchuria.

With his professional military sensitivities, Wainwright reckoned that the transfer to Manchuria held special significance, but he thought that the war would only be won when the Allied forces landed in Japan, which he guessed wouldn't happen until the end of 1946.

But Wainwright's conservative guess was formed in ignorance of what was going on in the wider world, where earth-shaking developments were taking place. The United States attacked the Marshall Islands on 31 January 1944. The US strategic bombing of the Japanese home islands got underway on 15 June. The Mariana Islands were secured by 10 August. On 20 October, six days after Wainwright and the other high-ranking POWs arrived in Manchuria, the Americans launched the four-month campaign to retake the Philippines. General MacArthur stepped ashore on the same day. Between 23 and 25 October, the Japanese were defeated in the Battle of Leyte Gulf. These were the battles that laid the foundation for the full capture of the Philippines and the subsequent capture of Okinawa.

The Japanese military began to unravel in 1944. But they still looked to the USSR-Japan Neutrality Treaty and to the Kwantung Army's abilities to forestall a Soviet invasion. The Kwantung Army began to prepare for war with the USSR. From February to September 1944, the Kwantung Army entered into a period of evolution towards conflict with the Soviet Union. From that October to the following March, the Kwantung Army devoted itself to preparations for a protracted war. From April to July 1945, the Kwantung Army's warfighting strengths further increased. As the end of the war drew near, the Kwantung Army adopted a plan to relinquish three quarters of Manchuria, withdraw to the mountainous Tonghua region in the southeast and fight a lengthy conflict against the Soviet forces. Since this put Xi'an county, originally buried deep in the Manchurian hinterland, close to the expected battle lines, the Japanese focused on an all-out struggle that used their senior military prisoners of war as bargaining chips.

On 17 March 1945, Japan's Army Ministry issued Order Number 2257, 'Regarding the Handling of Prisoners of War In Accord with Evolving Circumstances'. Its contents were these:

Guiding Principles:
 – Make all efforts to prevent the prisoners from falling into enemy hands. If necessary, move them.
 – If absolutely necessary, under enemy attack, release the prisoners.

Key Orders:
 – Strengthen the policing of all prisoner-of-war camps.
 – Regarding the moving of prisoners of war: as war conditions change, aerial attacks intensify, and the possibility of landings on our main islands looms, make careful studies of the placement of all prisoners of war and move or concentrate the prisoners according to what is learned.

141

Plans for the Movement of POWs:

   – Flexibility in movement and labour assignments.

   – Concentration of POWs.

   – If the situation is extremely urgent and above-mentioned plans for moving the POWs cannot be executed, free the prisoners.

   – Under the above conditions, give priority in moving the POWs to those capable of performing labour, those with strong constitutions, and those with the rank of general or colonel. But for those who resist, lose no opportunity to employ extraordinary measures, even if temporarily.

   – In releasing any prisoners, pay attention to avoiding harm to the local population.

   – Any special measures taken to suppress unrest or resistance must not provide ammunition for enemy propaganda or pretexts for revenge.

   – In arranging food supplies amid these conditions, make sure to provide at least the minimum necessary for sustaining POWs' lives in situations where normal transportation lines are disrupted.

From these orders, we can see that the Japanese forces were preparing to move to the western mountains and that the POWs were in extreme danger. The Japanese closed the camp at Zhengjiatun on 21 May and moved the remaining Allied officers and troops to the Mukden POW camp.

If the Japanese transfer of highly-ranked POWs to Taiwan two years earlier was for purposes of holding their positions and awaiting opportunities to launch counterattacks, the transfer of these prisoners to Manchuria reflected the gradual retreat of the Japanese and their decision to stake everything on one final and desperate plan.

Many biographies of General Wainwright tell the same story. A Japanese reporter came to the POW camp for an interview and asked him: "Do you expect to be court martialled when you return to the United States?" Wainwright told the reporter that he had never had that thought, because "a just country cannot judge a superior officer who issues a rational order on the field of battle". Wainwright's reply left the reporter disappointed. In fact, when Wainwright returned to the United States after the war, not only did he not face a court martial; he was quickly promoted and appointed commander of the Second Service Command and the Eastern Defense Command. Is it difficult to know what Wainwright's true feelings were? Could he have unburdened himself freely about his military successes or failures?

Wainwright's nephew Peter told me: "He still carried a heavy weight in his heart. In fact, he did not need to feel guilty at all, but you and I cannot understand his feelings at the time. He was a soldier, an army commander, and he believed that you should win on the battlefield, not fail."

## 14

# LIBERATION

By JULY 1945, with the surrender of the Japanese forces a more and more real possibility, Allied leaders became increasingly concerned over the welfare of the prisoners of war. They were particularly worried that the prisoners might be subjected to extreme treatment at the moment of the Japanese capitulation. With this in mind, the American commander in China, General Wedemeyer, ordered the Office of Strategic Services to organise small humanitarian liaison and assistance teams, under the command of the US 14th Air Force. These teams were assembled at Kunming and began training for their missions of rescuing prisoners of war. Their training complete, they set out from their base at Xi'an in northwest China.

The warrior units consisted of small teams of six men, known as 'Mercy Missions'. Their assignment, which covered the entire Chinese war zone, was to parachute into the prison camps, send in basic information about the condition of the prisoners and make sure that the prisoners would not be harmed while they were being liberated. They were also to gather evidence and serve as witnesses to any Japanese war crimes and violations of the Geneva

Convention. Finally, they were to secure airfields for the evacuation of personnel.

Each team included a medical corpsman, a communications soldier, a Japanese interpreter (usually a Japanese American) and a Chinese interpreter assigned by the Chinese army. Each team had a code name and designated military location. These code names and locations were: Operation Grey Duck – Wei Xian (present-day Weifang, Shandong province); Operation Magpie – Beiping (present-day Beijing); Operation Flamingo – Harbin (this operation was later temporarily suspended); Operation Sparrow – Shanghai (unsuccessful because the team was detained by the Japanese); Operation Pigeon – Hainan; Operation Seagull – Hankou; Operation Albatross – Guangdong; Operation Canary – Taiwan; Operation Quail – Hanoi, Vietnam; Operation Crow – Vientiane, Laos; Operation Golden Eagle – Seoul, Korea (later cancelled after Allied landings on the Korean peninsula); and Operation Cardinal – Mukden.

In August, General Edward King wrote in his diary:

10 Aug. Up until past two o'clock this morning on air raid drills. My room instead of the library the assembly point. Out twice to the shelter. The civilians must be impressed for we could see no lights anywhere around. Several drills today.

12 Aug. We were told at noon that we are to move and that our heavy baggage must be packed this afternoon. One report indicates we are to move northward which is hard to understand. The optimists think it is the end of imprisonment. I think it is too soon for that.

At 4.30am on 16 August, less than 17 hours after the Emperor's broadcast to the Japanese people announcing Japan's surrender, the Operation Cardinal team set out from Xi'an in a B-24 'Liberator' bomber on its mission to Mukden. The Mukden camp still lay under the strict control of the Japanese military, so it was not yet clear whether Operation Cardinal would succeed.

The B-24 Liberator was piloted by 21-year-old Paul Hallberg. The members of the Operation Cardinal rescue team were Major James T Hennessy (Special Ops team leader), Major Robert F Lamar (physician), Technician Edward A Starz (radio operator), Staff Sergeant Harold B Leith (Russian and Chinese linguist) and Sergeant Fumio Kido (Japanese interpreter). Cheng Shih-wu, a Chinese national, accompanied the team as an interpreter.

Team member Harold 'Hal' Leith remembered enjoying the view as he flew. "Looking at it, the scenery was very beautiful. I saw the Great Wall. I saw beautiful farmland, a beautiful country. I was praying that I could save the prisoners of war and take them home safely," he said.

Leith had volunteered for this mission. The principal languages in use at Mukden at that moment were Chinese and Russian, and Leith had just gained a grasp of both. He had completed parachute training at Kunming in May. "After the atomic bombs had been dropped on Hiroshima and Nagasaki, we thought that the war was coming to an end," said Leith. "We learned that if the Japanese surrendered, they might kill the prisoners of war, so we were very worried about the situation. General Wainwright and others were there, and they asked me to help rescue him."

At 10am, the plane neared Mukden. Hallberg reported a wind speed of 25 miles per hour and asked the team leader, Major Hennessy, whether the men would parachute. Winds like that could cause trouble for the parachutists, but Hennessy, mindful that liberating the POWs was the top priority, ordered them to jump.

Leith recalled: "We sat around a hole in the bottom of the plane and then jumped. I was the fourth one to jump. After jumping out, I heard the sound of my parachute opening. It was a wonderful sound to hear!" The smooth opening of their parachutes meant things were off to a good start. "I looked down and saw a group of Chinese farmers working in the fields. They stopped their work and looked up as if they were enjoying an aerial performance," said Leith.

At this time, the B-24 plane wheeled back and dropped supplies by parachute. These included items that the Operation Cardinal team needed: food, medicines, communications gear, etc. Just as the bomber was leaving the area, a Japanese fighter rose to pursue it. "It flew towards our plane but apparently did not carry any ammunition. It seemed to be preparing for a suicide attack," recalled the B-24 pilot, Paul Hallberg. He saw the Japanese fighter diving towards him and pulled the B-24 into a steep climb. The Japanese fighter brushed past the belly of the B-24 before it disappeared. "The Japanese soldier sitting in the cockpit looked up and was very annoyed that he had missed us," said Hallberg. The B-24 returned safely.

After that near miss, the Operation Cardinal team landed safely, and they quickly gathered in their parachutes. Some Chinese people came to help. The team explained to the Chinese why they had come and asked where the prison camp was. One of the Chinese stepped forwards to show them the way, so the team divided in two, one group staying on the scene to guard the supplies, while the other, including Leith and three others, set off for the POW camp with their Chinese guide.

As the team members moved towards the camp, a Japanese soldier suddenly appeared in front of them, armed with a rifle fitted with a bayonet. He knelt and took aim at the team. Leith saw that Lamar, standing by his side, was about to draw his weapon, and he stopped Lamar, saying: "If you make a move, I'll get you myself." Lamar did not do anything hasty. Just at that moment, another Japanese soldier came out of hiding just to the left and front of the team.

The team tried to tell the Japanese troops that the war was over. But the Japanese did not believe them. The Japanese blindfolded

147

them and led them to a small building. With their bayonets, the Japanese kept the men from talking to one another. Leith recounted: "While my eyes were covered, I was a little scared. I didn't know what they were going to do. I had seen photos in which they had used knives to cut off human heads, so there was some fear."

A little later, the men who had remained on the field guarding the team's supplies were also brought to the same building. The group numbered only five; the Chinese member of the team had disappeared. Leith guessed that he ran off because he was worried that the Japanese would dispose of him. The Japanese telephoned their superiors, and the Operation Cardinal team was then taken to Kempeitai headquarters, in a building across from the Daiwa Hotel in the centre of Mukden city.

When they reached Kempeitai Command, a Japanese colonel in charge had already received a phone call with some news, but he said that he hadn't yet received any instructions about surrendering. But he told the rescue team that from that moment forth they were not prisoners of war. "We seemed to have become the first prisoners of war released by the Japanese," said Leith.

When the camp rescue team demanded to go forwards to the camp, the Japanese colonel indicated that they could go, but that Colonel Matsuda, the officer in charge at the camp, would not allow them to enter the facility because he had not yet received formal orders. Finally, in the face of the team's firmness, the Japanese colonel agreed that the Americans could go to the camp, and sent the team's Japanese-American interpreter, who had just been apprehended, to accompany the men. He instructed the Japanese soldiers to make sure nothing happened to the team.

As the rescue team approached the main gate of the camp, the commandant, Colonel Matsuda, was waiting for them. But Matsuda refused to allow them inside the camp, and insisted that they not talk to anyone but him; all questions would be handled by Matsuda himself.

Leith recalled: "I looked up and saw some prisoners of war next to the window. I made an 'OK' gesture and waved at them." Then Colonel Matsuda had the team sent to the Daiwa Hotel, while he contacted Tokyo for further instructions.

Although formal news of the surrender still had not arrived, strange things had been happening over the past few days, and the numerous rumours going around that the war would be ending had put the POWs on edge. As the prisoners, always on the alert, caught scent of the drama unfolding just outside the camp gates, they quickly realised that something unusual was underway.

Robert Peaty recorded in his diary:

15 August 1945: The air-raid alarm went at about 9.30am, followed by the "All-clear" about half-an-hour later. The M.K.K. workers all returned after lunch, and No.1. Branch camp arrived a little later. The Chinese say the war is over. Colonel Marshall (U.S.A.) died this morning. Three-and-a-half years a Prisoner-of-War today.

16 August 1945: Funeral of Colonel Marshall. No.11. Branch Camp came in this afternoon. Six men were brought into camp this evening, and from the fact that they were smoking more than the regulation distance from an ash-tray, we knew they were not Prisoners-of-War. After an unusually good supper, all prisoners were released from the guard-house. Red Cross good supplies are to be "inspected" tomorrow.

On the morning of 17 August, after a restless and tormented night, the liberation team got off to a very early start. Though the Japanese had not treated them as POWs and had in fact made decent overnight arrangements for them, they had not for a moment forgotten their mission – the liberation of their brothers inside the camp. The first thing they did was go to the headquarters of the

Kempeitai. A colonel there told them that contact had been established with Tokyo and that they could go to the camp. The colonel further said that he was prepared to surrender formally to the camp liberation team at that very spot and that he wished to commit ritual suicide: did the liberation team wish to watch? The team told him that that was not necessary at that time; he was to remain there and assist in the liberation of the camp.

Then the camp liberators rode, in a car arranged by the Kempeitai, straight to the main gate of the camp. They entered immediately into the office of camp commander Matsuda. Matsuda appeared out of sorts; he had never seen so many Americans behaving so freely within his precincts, not even bowing before him. After a brief conversation, the Americans made clear that they wished to meet directly with the highest-ranking Allied prisoner in the camp. Matsuda said that he had already sent someone to call the prisoner.

After a few minutes, the door opened, and the American POW Major General George Parker stepped in. As soon as he entered, Parker saw General Matsuda and bowed before him. At that, Leith rushed to Parker and said: "General, do not bow; they have already surrendered to us. We will be sending everyone home."

Parker was elated. Leith opened the window and saw a crowd of POWs, at once agitated and timid, craning their necks for a glimpse of the room.

Leith knew that these men had been in Japanese hands for more than three years; how eager they must be to learn of the outcome of the war. "I needed to go out and tell them what was happening, and tell them that they would be going home," he said. Leith stepped out into the corridor and found himself facing several hundred POWs. He waded in among them and said in a powerful voice: "You are going home! The war is over! The Japanese have surrendered to us!" At first, the prisoners were silent. In the three years and four months since their capture on Bataan, Leith was the first free and strong American they had seen. Leith recalled: "When the prisoners first saw me in the camp, all of them were skinny, their faces looked bad, they were very hungry, and some were suffering with illness. My hair was red and, as a paratrooper, my body was strong, so they didn't use my name at all, but instead called me 'Big Redhead'."

Everyone – Americans, Dutch, British – swarmed happily around Leith. Finally, they found their voices with countless questions: Who won the 1943 and 1944 Rose Bowl championships? Is Roosevelt really dead? When did the war end? Who is the British prime minister? Is Wilhelmina, Queen of the Netherlands, still alive? How much do the different ranks get paid now? "Truly, this was the happiest day of my life," said Leith.

Escorted by the POWs, Leith made a quick inspection of the entire camp. He discovered the great size of the camp; that the barracks were overcrowded and disordered and overridden with fleas; that the POWs' bedding consisted of rice straw on wooden planks. Everywhere he went, the prisoners hailed him as a 'hero', which made Leith uncomfortable. As Leith put it: "They were the real heroes. From the battlefield to becoming prisoners, they experienced a more dangerous and cruel war."

After inspecting the camp, the liberation team returned to Matsuda's office. They had found no sign of General Wainwright. The team was upset; not finding Wainwright meant that the mission had not been accomplished.

From further interrogation of Matsuda, the team learned that Wainwright was being held at a different location, called Xi'an county, 150 kilometres northwest of Mukden. This was the Number Two Branch Camp, under the jurisdiction of the Mukden camp authorities. A total of 34 prisoners were held there, including Wainwright. When they learned of this, the camp liberation team changed their plans and decided to send Leith, who spoke Russian, and Lamar, the medic, to Xi'an to find Wainwright and the others.

All this time, the liberated prisoners in the Mukden camp

continued to celebrate. By then, the prisoners had taken over the entire camp, and General Parker, the most senior figure among them, took command.

Thousands of letters from home addressed to the prisoners and held by the Japanese were now handed to the former POWs. Sixty-five bags of mail were found, most of it two years old or more.

Major Peaty recorded what he saw and heard throughout those days, in excited diary entries:

18 August 1945: Our "liberators" are displaying remarkable efficiency. They arrived in a B-24 after a flight of over 1,000 miles, and as the big plane could not land on the airfield, they jumped. They brought with them their own equipment, which was also dropped by parachute, including a generating set, petrol, and all the components of a radio station. This was assembled yesterday, and our pressing needs were being sent out. At about 9pm, the message was picked up by a U.S. destroyer, and we understand that food and other supplies will be flown in. A pair of Japanese socks and a towel were issued all round, and British boots to those in need.

19 August 1945: Radio news is now coming in, and we learn that the Japanese in Manchuria are surrendering to the Russians. 14,000lb of necessities arrived by plane this morning, but the Russians have not allowed them to unload. It is most noticeable that the small amount of Red Cross food which remained now makes all the difference in the world to us.

20 August 1945: We believe that U.S. Hospital Ships are on their way to evacuate Prisoners-of-War, but there is no indication as to whether British and Dutch will be taken on them. At about 7pm, a small party of Russian officers arrived and announced that we are now "Svobodo" (free) and that they would enter into conference

with our senior officers at once to discuss details regarding our departure. Later in the evening, the Japanese guards were disarmed on the parade ground, and headed by their Colonel, they were marched in single file right around, guarded by us, now wearing their equipment and armed with their weapons, and escorted into their own guard-house in front of every man in camp. The Russian officer in charge said "Here they are – do what you like with them, cut their throats or shoot them, it is all the same to me", but this was translated diplomatically as "He says he hands them over to you". One Russian artillery officer to whom I spoke, told me that they were using 300 guns to the mile of front.

Although the Operation Cardinal team had liberated the camp on 17 August, the formal date of the camp's liberation was 20 August. As specified in the Yalta Agreement, the Soviet Union declared war on Japan on 8 August and the next day began moving troops into northeastern China, launching their Operation August Storm against the Japanese. In less than a month, the Soviet forces demolished the Kwantung Army. The Red Army liberated Mukden on 20 August and set up a Mukden Garrison. They assumed control of existing organisations and occupied the airport, the rail lines, the radio station and other important targets. They also liberated the Mukden POW camp. The Yalta Agreement specified that northeast China was to be placed under Soviet control; thus, formally speaking, the surrender of Japanese forces was offered to the Soviet Red Army.

The American POW Robert Rosendahl recalled that a Russian officer stood on a concrete platform at the hospital and made a speech to the POWs which was translated by a Russian speaker. Rosendahl was impressed as the officer talked about how powerful the Russian army was and how fast its actions were. Finally, he told the POWs that they were free from that moment on; Rosendahl never forgot that sentence.

Once the prison camps set up by the Japanese army in the various Pacific war zones were liberated, the Americans assembled a gigantic B-29 fleet on Okinawa. The 20th Bombing Group took on the task of air-dropping relief supplies to the Allied POWs. Over the entire span of the relief effort, 4,470 tons of supplies were delivered by air.

Allen, the American POW, recalled that the sight of the B-29s again was met with happiness and excitement, in contrast to the previous winter when they provoked tension and fear. Everyone was happy to be busy with responsibilities such as maintaining order, collecting the materials and transporting them to the prison camp.

But the air-drop operation did not start smoothly. While the aircrews had clear instructions about where to drop their goods outside the camp, they didn't pay close attention to their briefings. Their counterparts on the ground already had the radios brought in by the camp's original liberators, but they did not call on the right channel, so air and ground were not in communication, and it was impossible to direct the drops to the right locations. In the face of this, the POW in charge of ground communication, Lieutenant Thurman R Mathews (Mukden POW #13), thought of a solution. He had some of the men take quantities of flour from the camp kitchen and 'write' the correct communication channel identifiers on the camp's parade ground, where the aircrews could read them. Quickly enough, air and ground were able to establish communication, and the work of air-dropping supplies moved ahead smoothly.

In his diary, Major Peaty wrote:

25 August 1945: Some more sick were flown out today. The relief supplies which have been brought in by plane have been very much appreciated. (Several planes a day flew over later and dropped tons of food and clothing: we had to ask them to stop!) Today, we received two packets of American cigarettes each, and

a large issue of sugar. A bottle of lager beer for each man was obtained locally.

29 August 1945: Four B-29s arrived in the late afternoon and dropped about 120 parachute loads of supplies.

The contents of these air drops soon grew more rich. In the beginning, the drops contained emergency items such as foodstuffs, medicines and medical equipment. But then they moved upscale to include all manner of goods, even cultural and entertainment items. It got to the point that military medical advice went out to the POWs to watch their food and drink intake, to prevent serious health problems that could arise from over-eating after such long periods of food deprivation.

As the various tasks inside the camp were carried out amid brighter and brighter spirits, people fretted about the men who had been sent out on the liberation mission to Xi'an county. The main camp was completely out of communication with Xi'an because the Japanese communication system was inoperable. Had the men arrived without difficulty? Could they safely free the prisoners there? Would they be able to bring their freed senior-ranked POWs safely back to Mukden? No one could know the answers.

Hal Leith described the entire process of finding and freeing General Wainwright and the other captured generals in his wartime diary. On 17 August, escorted by an armed Japanese group, Leith and Lamar travelled about 150km by train to the camp in Xi'an, which was on a hilltop on the east side of the city.

When they arrived at the camp, Leith and Lamar were given camp beds to sleep on, and the Japanese made arrangements for them to meet with Wainwright and some of the other senior POWs. The Japanese commander of the camp was a graduate of an American university, so they had no problems communicating with him. The commander had received word that the Japanese had surrendered and was fully cooperative. There were about thirty POWs in the camp including high-ranking Americans, British and Dutch.

When Leith finally met with General Wainwright, he discovered that Wainwright was fearful about being seen as a traitor by the American people, because General MacArthur had told him that he must not surrender to the Japanese. Leith told Wainwright the American people recognised that if he hadn't surrendered, all of the POWs would now be dead and that he was a hero, not a villain. Leith discovered that it was Wainwright's 62nd birthday the very next day, 23 August 1945, so he had a cake made with some supplies that had come from the International Committee of the Red Cross.

The Japanese would not let the prisoners leave at that point, so Leith stayed with them while Lamar went back to Shenyang to make arrangements. During his time at the Xi'an camp, Leith played chess with Sir Mark Aitchison Young, the British governor of Hong Kong. After about a week, some large trucks with red flags entered the city; Leith reported to General Wainwright that they were probably Russians and that he would go down and speak with them. Leith and the Japanese camp commander met a Russian general, who was shocked to hear an American speaking fluent Russian. The Russian sent a squad of his men up to the camp to transport the prisoners to Shenyang on some buses that were provided by the Japanese.

On the long journey back to Shenyang, they stopped off at a village where the local Chinese fed them. Some of the roads on the way back to Mukden were slippery, and there were several occasions when the buses came off to the sides. They managed to get the buses back on the road with the help of the local Chinese. After two days of travelling in difficult conditions, the Russians agreed to let them complete the journey by train. After arriving in

Shenyang, Leith took Generals Wainwright, King and Moore to the airport where they boarded a C-47.

On 31 August, as he arrived in Japan, Wainwright said:

> Boy, this is what I've been waiting for for three and a half years. I couldn't be happier. Tonight in Yokohama, again a free American officer with a weapon in my hand, my heartfelt gratitude goes out to the American people, the administration and War Department, for the generous and sympathetic understanding of the dire misfortune which befell me in the Philippines in May of 1942. Through the kindness and generosity of my great commander, General Douglas MacArthur, I am here to witness on Sunday the greater misfortune of my enemy.

The formal signing of the Instrument of Surrender took place on the US Battleship Missouri in Tokyo Bay on 2 September 1945. After General MacArthur, representing the Allies, signed the document, he turned and handed the two pens he had used to two emaciated generals standing behind him. These were the two generals just liberated by the Operation Cardinal team from the Mukden POW camp: the American General Jonathan M Wainwright and the British General Arthur E Percival.

# THE FINAL STOP

ONCE THEY WERE FREED, the prisoners went through a period of agitation, but they soon sank into inexpressible and impenetrable feelings of sadness. They had yearned to go home for so long; now, listening to country music all day long, their hearts were already taking the first steps on their return voyage.

In actuality, arrangements for the evacuation of the prisoners from the camp were enmeshed in all sorts of improvised planning. According to the removal plan, the prisoners with the most urgent medical needs would first be flown to American military bases in Xi'an and Kunming for treatment. The first batch of 29 urgent-care cases left Shenyang on a B-24 on 24 August. Next, a group of higher-ranking prisoners were placed on the name list for evacuation; once freed, they received orders to return to duty at various locations. Over a period of ten days, 197 ailing prisoners and 41 senior officers, plus their attendants, took those urgent flights out of Shenyang.

It was impossible to evacuate large numbers of soldiers, but the resources needed to support those who had not yet been evacuated were improving day by day. The freed men understood that they would have to wait their turn.

There were two reasons for this: firstly, transport resources were inadequate, and the receiving units in Xi'an and Kunming were not able to handle the numbers of people involved; secondly, because of the tensions between the US and Soviet militaries, the Soviets stopped servicing US Navy ships at the port of Lvshun.

The plan at the time was for the remaining 1,300 prisoners, not including the urgent cases evacuated by air, to be removed by land and sea, with the US sending a troop transport to Lvshun – the military harbour nearest to Shenyang – to receive the POWs. But once the Soviet forces entered China's northeast and launched their August Storm offensive, all major matters in that part of China fell under Soviet final authority.

The Soviet forces faced a number of challenges. The announcement of Japan's unconditional surrender had not reached every Japanese unit stationed in northeast China, and Japanese forces were continuing to resist. In effect, the Japanese forces had not actually surrendered. Suicide squads, in particular, were inflicting casualties on the Soviet units. The Soviet armies were continuing to advance on the enemy.

The Soviet capture of Lvshun on 23 August brought the military conflict to a close. But the immediate follow-on work, especially involving details as to who would receive what in the war's aftermath, vexed all parties. The Soviets were too busy to pay much attention to the POW problem. That was the main reason for the slowdown in both the Americans' and the Soviets' dealing with the POW evacuation.

Furthermore, petty frictions – quarrels, drunken brawls and the like – soon broke out between the Soviet and American troops inside Shenyang itself. Though these were isolated incidents, they stemmed from the different military cultures of the two forces, and from deeper unprincipled conduct. Because the POW evacuation depended on a high degree of cooperation between the Americans and the Soviets, these individual incidents could not be taken lightly.

In the short period that ensued, the prisoners, who were totally focused on getting home, had no choice but to wait. For these men, who had lived for so long on the edge of life and death, this was desperately dispiriting.

During the first few days of their liberation, when the Red Army had not yet occupied Mukden, conditions outside the walls of the camp remained disordered. Small skirmishes and sniper fire happened constantly. Major Peaty wrote of one small episode on 23 August:

> Last night there was a considerable amount of rifle-fire in the vicinity, and this morning about fifty Japanese were trying to get into camp for protection from the Chinese. We had to put twenty extra men on guard. Warm clothing was issued, as the journey by air is likely to be at a high level and pretty cold, but as yet there is no news of evacuation starting.

These Japanese troops tried to surrender to the POWs, fearing that if they surrendered to the Red Army they would be sent to Siberia, but also fearing that the Chinese would take revenge on them. Of course, they couldn't succeed. They could only angrily depart. Under chaotic conditions like this, any official venture beyond the walls of the camp required authorisation from the senior officer inside the walls, General Parker. Private forays out of the camp were strictly forbidden. Prisoners who hoped to get outside to enjoy themselves were disappointed.

By the last week of August, conditions in Shenyang had begun to settle down. But the POWs still had no information about their evacuation. By this time, the POWs were permitted to go beyond the camp walls, in groups. Every day, knots of three to five men went into Shenyang to enjoy themselves. They could go no further than the lines of vendors' stalls at the street markets.

These slow days of waiting to go home gave the POWs the chance to get out of the camp, stroll through Shenyang, and thus to enter China itself and celebrate victory with their Chinese friends.

Once they were allowed out of the camp, the POWs surged out, looking for souvenirs to take home. Most popular of all were Japanese soldiers' swords. Some took Japanese *sanpachi shiki hohei-ju* military rifles.

Unlike many of his comrades, the American POW James Bollich did not venture into Shenyang in those first days of freedom. Instead, he went to the MKK plant where he had worked. Inside the plant, he was astounded at what he saw. "The entire plant was completely empty. Not a bit of machinery was to be seen," he said. Later, he learned that all the machinery had been seized and removed by the Red Army as spoils of war. Bollich could not avoid a certain disappointment, even anger. "It was no wonder that the trains that were to transport us home had been delayed," he said.

One day, Bollich and three or four of his comrades went to a park and discovered the monument displaying the remains of the engine of one of the B-29s the Japanese had brought down. They could not help recalling the terrifying days of heavy bombing months before. This time, they encountered a Soviet soldier, bottle in hand, who drunkenly proposed that they walk together. The Americans and British comrades did not feel particularly friendly and decided to get away from the Russian soldier, so they took off quickly. The Soviet soldier followed them with his eyes, then raised his rifle and opened fire. Luckily, Bollich and his friends got away unscathed. Perhaps because of what he had seen inside the empty MKK factory, Bollich got into repeated conflicts with Soviet troops whenever he went into Shenyang after that.

As soon as he was able to get outside the camp, the American POW Roland Towery went looking for Ge Qingyu, his Chinese friend at the MKK plant. Towery was overjoyed to be a guest at Ge's home and went touring through Shenyang with Ge's family. They all exchanged messages as souvenirs. In his message, Towery wrote: "Ge Qingyu is the friend and benefactor of the American prisoners of war. I hope that all American friends will treat him as kindly as he treated us."

After he was liberated, Oliver Allen kept thinking about one particular person. Cook Wang was the man in the MKK kitchen who had lost his job trying to protect Allen and other POWs. Allen and his friends tried everything and finally managed to find Wang. They invited him to return to the camp to cook. "We had to give him back his job to repay him for what he did for us," said Allen.

Robert Rosendahl had sought to stay out of trouble by keeping his distance from the others. What he did not anticipate, though, was that he would encounter one of his Chinese friends on one of his forays into Shenyang. Rosendahl recalled: "I came out of the prison camp and went to Shenyang city. A young doctor came to me and practised his English. His English was very good. He took me to his lab and showed me a penicillin sample that he was developing. It was a new drug that many people needed. He was very proud of it."

Rosendahl said that the Chinese doctor let them have a look at the cadaver samples in his laboratory. "I remembered that many prisoners of war had spoken about the Japanese doing human bacteria experiments. I don't know whether this took place in the prison camp, but my comrades often talked about it," he said. The young doctor led Rosendahl around the city and showed him the public water supply system. Later, they went to a beautiful Catholic church.

Li Lishui, who had worked at the MKK plant, lived at a place called 'Sang Family Graves'. This spot used to be a cemetery, but as people fled from northern China within the Great Wall to this place and settled there, it gradually became a small-scale concentration of

Chinese residents. It stood along the northern edge of the POW camp, separated from it by a man-made canal whose two banks were connected by a small stone bridge. Once the POWs were liberated, they often crossed over to the far side of the canal to enjoy themselves. With Japan's surrender, the MKK plant shut down. Li Lishui, idled at home, could stroll daily over to the main gate of the POW camp, where a crowd of Chinese usually gathered to watch the passing scene.

One morning at about nine o'clock, Li Lishui stepped out of his house in the usual manner and walked over towards the camp. He had just reached the little bridge over the canal when he spied a group of freed POWs strolling his way. Suddenly, one of the men called out in a loud voice, "Hello! Hello!" and rushed towards Li Lishui. Li realised that the man was POW number 266, Neil Gagliano, Li Lishui's 'cucumber friend'. Though they did not share a language, they met as two who had suffered together. Their joy and emotion transcended all boundaries, and they were thrilled to be reunited. When they finally parted, Gagliano pulled a handful of sweets from his pocket and gave them to Li Lishui.

It was not only the POWs who were idly waiting around. So were the men of Operation Cardinal. Hal Leith recorded in his diary that he had very little to do as he waited in Shenyang in late August and early September 1945. He was told by some of the British and Dutch officers that his team would be receiving awards from their respective counties. Some Americans working on public relations arrived from Kunming and said that the rescue mission had been a truly special action. The medic Lamar said that Leith's decision to stay in Xi'an county was crucial to bringing back the prisoners safely. When Leith ventured out in the city, he witnessed looting by the Russian soldiers and some violence from some of the local Chinese towards the Japanese. At one point, Leith intervened to prevent a Japanese child from being attacked.

Although the POWs were now making their way out of

Shenyang, a great many urgent tasks – both preparatory and follow-up in nature – remained there. On 29 August, US Army Headquarters China sent a team to Shenyang; the group was called the 'POW Recovery Team'. The 19 team members were under the command of Major James F Donovan of the Office of Strategic Services, a wartime US intelligence agency. The team's main job was to handle preparations for the departure of the POWs and to manage all related follow-up matters. They built a registry of all the POWs and handled medical examinations, along with immunisations. In addition, they were assigned the job of sorting out the facts at all POW burial sites, certifying the identity of all remains, registering them and exhuming them in preparation for repatriation of the deceased to their families. Other vital tasks emerged for the team as well. POWs were interviewed for the record, and witness testimony was taken regarding Japanese suspected of crimes. This was in preparation for post-war war crimes trials.

By early September, Soviet military activity in northeastern China was wrapping up. The Soviets agreed to provide rail transport and port services to facilitate the evacuation of the Allied prisoners.

In fact, the Soviet military paid close attention to the evacuation of the Allied prisoners, assigning Major Alexander Pritula to handle the process. In addition to providing rail transport from Shenyang to Lvshun for the evacuation, they broke precedent and allowed a US military transport ship to dock at the port of Lvshun to receive the POWs.

The first contingent of 752 American, British and other Allied POWs left Shenyang by train for Lvshun on 10 September 1945. A day later, the remaining 631 prisoners reached Lvshun. One group boarded the US Navy hospital ship named Relief, and the other boarded the brand-new troop transport, USS Colbert. After leaving Lvshun, they passed through Okinawa and Manila on their way back to the United States. But in the middle of the repatriation, the

Colbert struck a mine near Okinawa, badly damaging its propellers and engine room. Just above the engine room were the quarters for the US Marines on board. William A C Frising (Mukden POW #1414), a member of the 4th US Marine Division, was killed in the explosion.

This young Marine suffered through three and a half years of captivity, only to give his life on his way home after waiting for so long.

The work of evacuating the Mukden POW camp came to an end on 19 September, after the remains of those who had perished were recovered. With that, the US Prisoner Recovery Team departed from Shenyang.

Allied prisoners from Europe also made their way home in stages. James Percival, the son of General Sir Arthur Percival, said: "My father returned to the UK by plane and then took a car home. My mother, my sister and I went to meet him. I saw that he was very thin and he looked very tired. After her got home, it took him a long time to recover. Our family was very happy to be reunited with him."

# 16

# THE SEARCH FOR SERGEANT LYNCH

IN A QUIET CORNER OF MANILA, far from the noise and bustle of the city's centre, there lies a US military cemetery holding the remains of American servicemen who died overseas. It is called the Manila American Cemetery and Memorial.

The cemetery encompasses 61,500 square metres and holds the remains of 17,206 soldiers – both officers and enlisted men. It is the largest American military cemetery outside of the United States. The core of the cemetery is a circular area, comprised of two semi-circular corridors. The corridors are supported by long marble colonnades, on which the names of 36,285 names are inscribed. They are the names of all those servicemen who remain missing from the Pacific war. According to American law at the time, servicemen who did not return to their units by the specified time were classified as 'Missing in Action'. One year after being declared Missing in Action, if no word of their whereabouts was forthcoming, they were declared dead.

Among the names of the missing servicemen inscribed at the Manila memorial is the name William Joseph Lynch. According to the official records of the US Office of Missing and Prisoners of

War, Lynch was a staff sergeant in the United States Marine Corps, serial number 256599, who enlisted in the armed forces in Dorchester, Massachusetts. He was declared dead on 21 May 1946.

On 3 May 1957, by approval of the city council in Lynch's home town, a small plot of land in Dorchester was designated the 'William Joseph Lynch Square' in order to commemorate this hero of the second world war. The Boston City Council Resolution specified that Lynch disappeared on 18 May 1944 while a Japanese prisoner of war and that the official date of his death was certified as 21 May 1946.

Thus William Joseph Lynch rested in history.

But neither the cool marble inscription in Manila listing the names of the Missing in Action nor the words on the small stone monument at the plaza in Massachusetts came close to telling the ending of Lynch's story.

Lynch was captured by the Japanese on Corregidor on 6 May 1942 and assigned prisoner number 607. He and the other prisoners reached Mukden on 11 November, and he was assigned to labour at the MKK plant. The materials show clearly that, on his POW registration card, his occupation was listed as "welder".

On 1 May 1944, the Japanese began construction of their second prison camp at the site of the Manshū Leather Company plant in the Tiexi district of Mukden. Lynch was one of 150 prisoners moved from the main camp to the new facility.

The night of 17 May was especially dark, amid drizzling rain. At 11.30, Lynch left his barracks to visit the toilets. Because the prisoners had only occupied the new camp for ten days, the toilets were still under construction, and the prisoners were using a temporary, hastily built shed. Lumber was stacked around the walls of the toilet shed. On his trip to the toilet, Lynch knocked out the shed window and used some of the lumber to make his escape. He scaled the three-metre wall, used some of the lumber to cross over the barbed wire, and made his 'jailbreak' under cover of darkness.

The night guard patrol discovered Lynch missing at midnight. At 12.30am, all the POWs were mustered for a roll call. The Kempeitai immediately sent two squads out to capture Lynch. One went to the Huanggutun railway station to apprehend him. The other searched along the rail line outside the camp. Some additional men from inside the camp were assigned to help in the search.

At 5.30am, the Japanese received a report that someone resembling a prisoner had been spotted about two thousand metres north of the Number One Dispatch Station, moving south along the rail line. At the same time, the main camp sent 24 men to bolster the squad at the Number One station, to make sure that the Number Two camp remained stable and under control. All prisoners who had remained in the camp were immediately interrogated severely. Everyone in Lynch's immediate prisoner group was placed under 'extra intense' scrutiny, while the head of Lynch's group and the seven prisoners closest to Lynch's bunk were punished in the 'heavy guard' warehouse. On 18 May, at a place about twenty kilometres northwest of Mukden, known as Masanjiazi, a group of local residents reported that they had discovered Lynch. The local police bureau sent policemen and local residents to surround him, and he was taken into custody.

Once Lynch was apprehended, the Kempeitai threw him into jail.

After the 'jailbreak incident', the Mukden POW camp sent three reports to the Prisoner Information Bureau in Tokyo, which was responsible for gathering and exchanging all information relating to prisoners of war. The reports detailed Lynch's escape, his capture and his subsequent sentencing. They read as follows:

Top Secret
Mukden Prisoner of War Camp Report No. 55
18 May 1944
On the escape of a prisoner (Report No. 1)

To: Director, Bureau of Prisoner Information
From: Director, Mukden Prisoner of War Camp

1. Escapee: William J Lynch, Staff Sergeant, US Marines, age 28, prisoner number 607.

2. Timeline: Normal work performance in factory on 17 May. At roll call (8.30pm) all prisoners accounted for. From 9.30pm to 10.30pm, a local guard performed a bed check on his usual rounds. All was normal. At midnight, the guard on his usual rounds received a report from the leader of one of the POW small groups that prisoner 607 was missing. The guard immediately reported this to Corporal Nakata, who was working in his office. Nakata called an urgent meeting, and a report was sent immediately to the camp commandant at his residence. A man was dispatched to report at once to the managers of the plant. At this time, 12.30am, the commandant ordered an immediate roll call and reported the event to the Kempeitai.

3. Circumstances of the escape: The nightwatchman at Barracks 245 says that at about 11.20pm on 17 May he saw the accused prisoner 607 returning from the toilet. This will require further investigation. It is possible that he used a window in the toilet facility (precautions had already been taken, but one window was badly damaged) or else the roof of the toilet structure (the toilets were under construction, and the toilet being used was a temporary structure) to escape from his barracks. Some of the scrap wood left over from the construction work was used to enable the escapee to get over the security wall (approximately three metres in height). We suspect that the escapee used other additional methods, but these have not been confirmed.

4. The escapee:

a) The escapee had earlier been confined for fifteen days because of bad conduct towards plant supervisory personnel, but since that time all had gone smoothly, and he was a diligent worker in the plant. On 2 May, when all the prisoners were dispatched to this camp, the escapee took a solemn oath that he would obey all regulations relating to the prisoners. Most of those regulations dealt with all communications with Japanese and with native Manchukuo people. Once assigned to this camp, the escapee's work was sober. (This was possibly aimed at averting others' suspicions of his plot.)

b) Dilapidated clothes. American-style work clothes (summer wear), US-made military boots. Wearing a US Navy cap. Also a backpack, but carrying very little money.

c) His comrades indicate that he was unusually quiet on 17 May, but that he was a man of few words in any case.

5. Measures taken after the event:

a) At 12.39am on 18 May, the commandant ordered an immediate and urgent roll call and contacted the Kempeitai. Accompanied by a translator, he went to the dispatching station. A search team of three men under the command of Lieutenant Fukushima went to the area of the Huanggutun railway station to search. Another team under Lieutenant Hayashi searched along the rail line around the Huanggutun station. They arrived at their assigned locations at 12.30am.

b) They worked together and cooperated with the Kempeitai when the latter arrived on the scene.

c) According to the report received from Lieutenant Hayashi at

5.00am, several Manchu children spied someone who looked like an escaping prisoner moving south along the rail line about two thousand metres northwest of the dispatch station. Impossible to confirm whether that person was the escapee. Awaiting further reports. Sent Captain Nakata and four men to confirm.

d) Sent four army officers, three non-coms and 17 local militia from the main camp to strengthen military security.

e) Conducted a thorough examination of all other prisoners remaining at the dispatch station.

6. Safety:

a) The guard contingent at the Number One Dispatch Station was under the command of Second Lieutenant Ando. In addition, there were NCO Sergeant Nakata and four local civilian security personnel, all on assignment from this office. The plant also arranged for five Japanese and five Manchukuo personnel. Their normal daily tasks were assigned by the military. Those personnel assigned by this Mukden POW Camp were divided into two teams.

b) As the toilet facility and bath house were still under construction, camp and factory personnel worked together on the toilet construction project. Security along the periphery of the toilet facility was extremely tight.

c) We had been in the process of training security personnel, as they are all new to their tasks. To this point, we have not yet completed their training.

7. The prisoners had been transferred here from the main camp ten

days earlier, and thus did not have full knowledge of the periphery of the site. From our knowledge of what the escapee had with him at the time of the escape, we can assume that the escape was not premeditated. Furthermore, we are in possession of letters of appreciation from other prisoners with respect to conditions here (we analysed the possibility that they were intentionally false, but concluded that they held substantial propaganda value). This case will be handled as an extremely serious criminal matter.

(End of Report No. 1)

Top Secret
Report on Mukden Case
Report on Apprehension of the Escapee (Report No. 2)
To: Director, Bureau of Prisoner Information
From: Commandant, Mukden Prisoner of War Camp

1. Escapee: William J Lynch, Staff Sergeant, US Marines, age 28, prisoner number 607.

2. Circumstances of apprehension: The accused went over the wall from the Number One Dispatch Station in a westerly direction, apparently at random, hoping to make his way to a US air base in China. The night was rainy and very dark, and the escapee lost his way but continued moving towards the northwest. At 11.15am on 18 May, en route to the northwest of Shenyang at Masanjiazi, he was spotted by a local resident. On receipt of that report, the police at Masanjiazi and a number of local residents surrounded the suspect and apprehended him.

3. Circumstances of the escape: We now have the report of the Kempeitai in the Tiexi district. The results of the interrogation of the suspect at our facility reveal the following. At 11pm on the 17 May, the suspect in his bunk secretly changed into summer clothes

and then went to the temporary toilet facility for his barracks (a wood-plank rain shed three metres in height). Stepping along the wooden planks, he crossed over the wall and found himself outside the barracks. He then came quickly to a pile of scrap wood left over from work on the construction of the toilet facility and used those pieces of lumber to go over the security wall, which was three metres in height and topped with three strands of barbed wire. Coming to the wall surrounding the factory, he escaped after crossing the barbed wire there. Guards on their rounds between 10.30pm and 11.00pm detected nothing unusual. At 11.20pm, Japanese personnel completed their rounds. The prisoner in charge of night duty recorded that he had just returned from the toilet and was standing across from the entrance to the door of the administrative office. (Recording the names of all those making trips to the toilet was an escape-prevention measure.)

4. Regarding the escapee: The accused was an especially quiet person, with many likes and dislikes. His manner was not stable. He was a hard worker in the factory but quickly took a disliking to his tasks. Once he began labour in the leather factory, however, he was a harder worker than the others. In the barracks, he liked to read (reading materials were carefully inspected and allowed only after approval while the reading room was under construction). During interrogation after his apprehension, he acknowledged that he had become increasingly fed up with his living conditions since the spring of the preceding year, expecting that the war would have ended with American victory by March. When this did not happen, he realised that the war could drag on much longer. His behaviour became more unstable, even to the point of suggesting mental breakdown. He buried himself in reading at the camp. The accused revealed that at the time of his escape he estimated his chances of success at one in five hundred.

5. Construction: Construction work at the Manshū Leather Company is proceeding vigorously to this day. But work on the toilet building and bath house was only about half finished. Because of difficulties in arranging the necessary units to do the work, the construction had been delayed. Construction materials had been piled nearby outside the security wall close to the construction site. These were ready made for use in scaling the wall. The shed housing the temporary toilet was another weak point. Although we are short of materials, we will take care of this as soon as possible.

6. Measures Taken:

a) Educational measures carried out among all prisoners at the dispatch station.

b) One week's punishment for all members of the escapee's small group.

c) Punitive incarceration for the head of that small group, the prisoner on night assignment and the prisoners to the right and left of the escapee's bunk.

(End of Report No. 2)

Top Secret
Via Kwantung Army Headquarters.
Mukden Prisoner of War Camp Report No. 60
To: Director, Prisoner Information Bureau
From: Commandant, Mukden Prisoner of War Camp
Prisoner Escape Report No. 3

1. Suspect: William J Lynch, Staff Sergeant, US Marines, age 28, prisoner number 607.

2. Interrogation of prisoners following the event: This prisoner was not sociable. His only friends were three or four fellow US Marines. After his arrest and interrogation by military personnel of the Mukden Prisoner of War Camp, he detailed the following:

a) Reason for his escape: The severe regime at the camp was ubiquitous, but he could no longer endure life in the camp. He assumed the end of the war was near.

b) At 11.20pm on 17 May, he went to the toilet. At the time, he did not have any thoughts of escape. After returning to his bunk, he suddenly came upon the idea of making his escape.

c) He did not ponder carefully the likelihood of success or failure. He only thought of making his way to an American air base. He assumed that the rain and dark of night would help him, and estimated his chances of success at one in five hundred.

3. General views of other prisoners regarding the accused: He was considered strange. His only friends in the camp were three or four other Marines.

4. Behaviour of all prisoners in this facility: Severe measures imposed after earlier escape attempts had proven effective, with the exception of this individual. The other prisoners were fearful of any further escape attempts. For example, after Prisoner #606 went to the toilet at 12.05am, he immediately reported to his group leader when he realised that someone was missing. From this, we conclude that neither in the main camp nor in this

dispatch station was any other prisoner involved with the suspect's escape. The other prisoners are all working normally.

5. Other information conveyed by the accused, over and above that concerning the escape:

a) Reason for joining the military: Soldiers must follow orders. Furthermore, everything else is easy; he wanted to enjoy an easy life, so he joined the military.

b) War fighting: A soldier has no other choice. Civilians can choose to do other things.

c) Feelings for his country: The common people are used by the small elite of capitalists. Democracy and freedom are phrases people like to hear, but the common people are just used as tools. Roosevelt is just a puppet seeking popularity.

d) Anti-English sentiments. He dislikes the English. They use the influence of the British Empire to oppress other races.

6. The above information was obtained during the criminal investigation or during the process of taking him into custody. We assess that his responses were designed to lighten his punishment and to make the Japanese happy.

7. Opinions of the Mukden camp commandant and measures taken: The escapee was not armed. Normally, the death penalty is indicated with a view towards influencing those prisoners who have not attempted to escape in the past. But seeing the apparent mental collapse of the accused, it is hoped that the punishment will instead be the longest possible term of imprisonment.

From these three reports, we can see that the Japanese treated the Lynch escape with the highest urgency and seriousness, making use of a variety of investigative agencies – the police, camp guard personnel and even the Kempeitai – both for searching and for investigation. The Japanese military used the Lynch escape for grounds to impose severe indoctrination and punitive measures on all other prisoners. All of this could not but remind the men of the escape attempt that had taken place a year before.

On 6 June 1944, a 'Provisional Military Conference' comprised of personnel from Kwantung Army headquarters sentenced Lynch to seven years in prison on the charge of violating the Prisoner of War Criminal Law.

The surviving American POW Roy Weaver said: "My prisoner number was 610. Lynch's was 607. We slept in the same wide bunk. Originally, prisoners 608 and 609 were between us. But later they both died." [Prisoner #608, Harry M Blaine, died at the camp on 12 January 1943; Prisoner #609, Clark A Savage, died at the camp on 24 December 1942]. Thus, Weaver and Lynch became immediate neighbours in the bunk. Weaver was also a Marine and became one of Lynch's few friends. When Lynch was assigned to the new Number One Dispatch Station in May 1944, Weaver remained in the main camp, and the two men were separated. "I saw Lynch being carried back to the prison camp on a stretcher. After that, I never saw him again," said Weaver. Lynch was detained briefly in the main camp and interrogated by Japanese army personnel, and then he simply disappeared.

From that point on, Lynch became nothing more than a name in a registry. Every day the prisoners attended roll call. Normally, each prisoner responded in a loud voice when his name was called. When Lynch's name was called, the head of his small group, at the orders of the Japanese, would call out: "In prison."

The last batch of POWs left Shenyang for the military port of Lvshun on the way home. That day, the US Army produced a report on the matter of Lynch, who had not returned to his unit and whose whereabouts were unknown. The report was prepared by US Army Colonel Stuart Wood. Aside from a brief account of Lynch's 'jailbreak', the body of the report dealt with the search for him.

Thenceforth, Lynch was officially listed as Missing in Action, the date of his disappearance set at 18 May 1944. On 21 May 1946, the US Army officially declared Lynch deceased, asserting that he died at the hands of the enemy while undertaking his duties, not through any errors of his own.

Lynch – unseen dead or alive – became the only Mukden POW camp prisoner to disappear forever. The mystery became a permanent source of lingering pain in the hearts of Lynch's family members. For the POWs, the mystery has lasted for seven decades. Lynch's fate also became a nagging concern for Chinese and foreign scholars. In my interviews with surviving Mukden prisoners, the matter of Lynch's disappearance was often a key topic.

In recent years, through a combination of oral recollections and printed sources, the circumstances surrounding Lynch's disappearance have gradually become more understood.

I began a cooperative effort with American scholars in October 2008, and we started work on Lynch's disappearance. I also conducted interviews with witnesses and on-site investigations, including the use of high-technology tools, and consulted with archaeologists and anthropologists. Our work proceeded slowly.

Everyone involved was dedicated to working for the cause of peace, regardless of where they had come from or where they had fought in the war. They were all heroes in a shared cause. Lynch was the same kind of hero. The American military has a saying: "Never abandon your comrades." Seventy years later, as comrades in the struggle against fascism, we still refused to abandon hope. Sending a hero back to his home was our duty.

# 17

# THE POST-WAR TRIALS

ON 2 SEPTEMBER 1945, Japan signed the Instrument of Surrender, accepting the detailed provisions contained in the Potsdam Declaration. This signified the formal, legal termination of armed hostilities in the Pacific war. But it opened up a whole new kind of conflict. Although this new struggle lacked the blood and violence of the military conflict, it was just as profound, for it involved the verdicts of the world in promoting justice; it had a far-reaching impact on the legacies of history; and it reflected the enormous complexity of war itself. This battle was over the legal actions necessary to carry out the Potsdam Declaration's call for "punishment of war crimes". It should be noted that Japan's signing of the surrender document confirmed its acceptance of the declaration, and provided the Allied Powers with the most basic foundation on which to apply the judicial processes to the actions of Japanese war criminals.

In the post-war trials, Japanese war criminals were divided into three categories. The Class A war criminals were those responsible for setting policy, secretly planning, organising and leading in committing "crimes against peace", "war crimes" and "crimes against humanity". Two hundred people, of whom Tōjō Hideki was the most senior, were designated as Class A war criminals. These were the top people who set the war of aggression in motion and laid down war policies.

Because their crimes affected many countries, they were subject to trial by the International Military Tribunal for the Far East. That tribunal considered "crimes against peace" to be the "greatest international crimes", comprehensively encompassing "all manner of damages".

The other two categories were known as Class B and Class C. They included "ordinary war criminals" – both leaders and those who carried out the abuse of prisoners of war or the slaughtering of civilians in contravention of the laws of war. According to the agreements worked out among Allied Powers, those accused of such crimes were to be tried by tribunals specific to the individual nations that suffered from their actions. Thus, in addition to the trials conducted in Tokyo by the International Military Tribunal for the Far East, the Allies conducted trials in a total of 49 war crimes courts in Beiping, Shanghai, Nanjing, Shenyang and Hong Kong, as well as in Manila, Singapore, Rangoon, Saigon and Khabarovsk, among other locations. The accused were tried on charges of "war crimes" and "crimes against humanity". A total of 5,730 Japanese were tried in these courts, of whom 4,490 were convicted and sentenced. Among the latter, 991 were sentenced to death.

The government of the Republic of China held trials in a total of ten cities, including Beiping and Shanghai, from late 1945. On 6 November, the government created the Commission for the Handling of War Crimes. Between August 1945 and May 1947, a total of 2,357 people were apprehended throughout the country. Detention centres were set up in ten cities specifically for Japanese war criminals. Special military courts for the trial of war criminals were established in Beiping, Shenyang, Nanjing, Guangzhou, Jinan, Hankou, Taiyuan, Shanghai, Xuzhou and Taibei between 16

December 1945 and 1 May 1946. A total of 871 defendants were convicted; of these, 147 were executed, 83 were sentenced to life imprisonment, 276 were sentenced to shorter terms and 365 were found not guilty.

In early 1946, the US China Theatre organised a military commission – a tribunal – in Shanghai, conducting ten trials involving 48 defendants between January and September of that year. The tribunal imposed six death sentences, nine life imprisonment verdicts and 28 sentences of various durations, and found five defendants not guilty. The trials of Matsuda Genji and Kuwashima Joichi, on charges of abusing prisoners at the Mukden POW camp, were conducted at the Huade Road prison in Shanghai.

The tribunal in the Matsuda and Kuwashima cases was established under Special Order 137 of the Nanjing Headquarters, US Army in China, on 20 August 1946. Paragraph 8 of that order specified that the War Department had authorised the US Army Nanjing headquarters on 3 July 1946 to create a military commission for the purpose of carrying out trials of those accused of war crimes. The military tribunal was comprised of people from the US Army, the Army Legal Department and other bodies.

Colonel Daniel H Mallan chaired the tribunal. Other tribunal members included Lieutenant Colonel James B Leer, Lieutenant Colonel C Radford Berry and Lieutenant Colonel Frederick W Stairwalt. Second Lieutenant William J Fuller Jr served as prosecutor. Lieutenant Raymond A Kirby handled administrative tasks. The military order commanded the tribunal to convene in Shanghai under its chairman and authorised the military commission to hire or assign appropriate interpreters, record-keepers, rapporteurs or other assistants.

The same military order commanded that the military commission it created would follow the "regulations for the trial of war crimes defendants", as established by the US Army China Command on 21 January 1946, in order to guarantee complete fairness in the treatment of individuals, units or organisations, and empowering the commission to establish other regulations for the conduct of the military trials, as dictated by circumstances.

Over a period of 11 days, from 5 to 16 September 1946, the military tribunal accumulated seven volumes of witness testimony, 35 volumes of testimony from the prosecution and investigatory authorities including written testimony from General Wainwright and other former Mukden POWs. The tribunal further carried out its own questioning of witnesses and heard various defence motions. A number of POWs offered testimony. The military tribunal returned its verdicts on 16 September 1946. The Legal Advisor Office of the US Army Military Advisory Group (MAG) in China reviewed these on 18 January 1947 and sent its report to the commander of the MAG.

The first part of that report paid special attention, on the basis of tribunal records, to the identities of two of the accused, the validity of the charges against them, the verdicts rendered, whether the accused had admitted their guilt and so on. The report concluded:

OFFENSES:

1) GENJI MATSUDA (Trans. Ex. #6)

CHARGE: That during the period of time between December 1942 and August 1945, while Japan was at war with the United States of America and its Allies, Genji Matsuda, Colonel, Imperial Japanese Army, as commanding officer of the Japanese prisoner of war camps in the vicinity of Mukden, Manchuria, did unlawfully disregard and fail to discharge his duty to accord to the American prisoners of war then confined in said prison camps, the treatment and protection to which prisoners of war were then entitled and did unlawfully fail to restrain the persons under his command from committing brutal atrocities and other high crimes

182

against the said prisoners of war then confined in the prison camps under his control, thereby contributing to the numerous deaths and prolonged illnesses among such American prisoners of war, in violation of the laws and customs of war.

BILL OF PARTICULARS: (Summarized)

1. Failed to provide adequate food, clothing, shoes, heat and housing conditions.
2. Failed to provide sufficient medicines, particularly those drugs needed for the treatment of dysentery and avitiminosis.
3. Failed to provide proper surgical care.
4. Failed to restrain persons under his command from committing brutal and inhuman beatings and other atrocities.
5. Failed to restrain personnel under his command from conducting numerous inspections of the American prisoners of war in sub-zero weather and exposing them to the elements in partly or wholly unclothed condition.
6. Caused or allowed numerous American prisoners of war to be confined for unreasonable periods of time.
7. Failed to provide necessary dental and eye treatment.
8. Caused or allowed numerous group restrictions and punishments to be imposed.
9. Permitted Joichi Kuwashima to brutally beat and torture Sergeant, then Corporal, Thomas R. Gagnet, American prisoner of war, by beating and kicking him about the head and body, by giving him the water treatment and by confining him in the guardhouse with wet clothing and without heat, water, food or bedding facilities.
10. Failed to prevent the medical officer of said camp from torturing sick patients by forcing them to stand barefoot

183

in snow and ice and caused to run around the parade grounds.

11. Failed to cause American prisoners of war to be advised of the innumerable rules and regulations of the said prisoner of war camps, thereby causing personnel under his command to beat and otherwise brutally torture American prisoners of war for alleged violations of said rules and regulations.

12. Unlawfully failed to prevent the illegal execution of three American prisoners of war who had escaped from camp.

13. Failed to cause prisoner of war camps to be designated as such so as to prevent attacks from air raids and failed to provide American prisoners of war with air raid shelters for protection against air raid attacks.

14. Failed to provide for the distribution of International Red Cross medicines and supplies received at the camps.

15. Failed to have the American prisoners of war treated in accordance with the requirements of the Geneva Prisoner of War Convention.

JOICHI KUWASHIMA, also known as Kawajima (Trans. Ex. #6)

CHARGE: That during the period of time between December 1942 and October 1944, while Japan was at war with the United States of America and its Allies, Joichi Kuwashima, also known as Kawajima, Captain, Imperial Japanese Army, the medical officer of the Japanese prisoner of war camps in the vicinity of Mukden, Manchuria, did unlawfully disregard and fail to discharge his duties as such medical officer, and did wilfully and unlawfully commit cruel, inhuman and brutal atrocities against the American prisoners of war then confined in the said prisoner of war camps, thereby contributing to the numerous deaths and prolonged illnesses among such American prisoners of war, in violation of the laws and customs of war.

BILL OF PARTICULARS: (Summarized)

1. Failed to make available sufficient medicines and drugs needed for the treatment of dysentery and avitiminosis.
2. Failed to provide proper surgical care for American prisoners of war by denying the use of hospital facilities to the prisoner of war medical staff.
3. Forced numerous American prisoners of war to stand inspections in sub-zero weather in partly or wholly unclothed condition.
4. Tortured numerous sick American prisoners of war by forcing them to stand barefoot in snow and ice and to run around the parade ground as an alleged diagnosis of their ailments.
5. Failed to make available for general use the International Red Cross medical supplies which arrived in said prisoner of war camps.
6. Failed to make available to Sergeant, then Corporal Thomas R. Gagnet and others the medical treatment and eyeglasses needed on account of failing eyesight.
7. Brutally tortured Sergeant Thomas R. Gagnet by beating him about the head and body with a cased saber and with his fist, by kicking him and giving him the water treatment and by confining him in the guardhouse without trial in extremely cold weather with his clothes still wet from the water treatment without food, water, or bedding for a period of two days.
8. Failed to provide sufficient anesthetic for the completion of an operation upon Corporal Edward S. Coley and did strike and abuse said prisoner of war.

PLEAS OF BOTH DEFENDANTS:

Not Guilty (R 7).

FINDINGS:

As to GENJI MATSUDA. Of the Charge GUILTY, except the words "and did unlawfully fail to restrain the persons under his command from committing brutal atrocities and other high crimes against the said American prisoners of war then confined in the prison camps under his control, thereby contributing to the numerous deaths and prolonged illnesses among such American prisoners of war". Of the excepted words, Not Guilty. (R 187)

As to JOICHI KUWASHIMA. Of the charge GUILTY except the words "the numerous". Of the excepted words, Not Guilty. (R 187)

SENTENCE:

As to GENJI MATSUDA: To be confined at hard labor at such place as the reviewing authority may direct for seven (7) years. (R 187)

As to JOICHI KUWASHIMA: Death by hanging at such place as the reviewing authority may direct. (R 187)

MAXIMUM SENTENCE:

As a military commission may direct.

CONVENING AUTHORITY:

Lieutenant General A. C. Gillon, Commanding General, Nanking Headquarters Command.

PLACE OF TRIAL:

Court Room in Ward Road Jail, Shanghai, China.

DATE OF TRIAL:

Arraignment: 5 September 1946

Interlocutory motions: 5 September 1946

Trial: 5 September 1946 to 16 September 1946 (R 1, 187)

PRELIMINARY REMARKS:

1. Pursuant to paragraph 8, Special Orders Number 137, Nanking Headquarters Command, dated 20 August 1946, a Military Commission was appointed for the trial of persons, units and organizations accused as war criminals and on completion thereof to transmit the record of trial, including any judgment or sentence, directly to this Headquarters for action by the appointing authority (Trans. Ex. #1). By letter of transmittal dated 20 August 1946, the charges against the two accused were forwarded by the Staff Judge Advocate to the Commanding General, Nanking Headquarters Command (Trans. Ex. #2). By first indorsement dated 20 August 1946, these charges were referred, to be tried in a common trial, by the Commanding General, Nanking Headquarters Command (Trans. Ex. #3) before the Military Commission appointed as above set forth.

2. Upon the inactivation of the Nanking Headquarters Command

on 28 October 1946, Chief, Army Advisory Group, was authorized by WD Radio WCL 34266, dated 5 December 1946, to review, approve and order executed sentences, including the death sentence adjudged by military commissions appointed by the Commanding General, Nanking Headquarters Command.

3. Both the preliminary investigation and the present record of trial reveal that other Japanese personnel were involved in the offenses charged against the accused. One Toru Miki, formerly a Captain in the Japanese Imperial Army was tried by a Military Commission appointed by the Commanding General, United States Forces, China Theater, and was on 14 March 1946 sentenced to confinement at hard labor for twenty-five (25) years, which said sentence was duly approved by the Commanding General, United States Army Forces China. Other Japanese personnel on the staff of the accused, Genji Matsuda, who had personally beat or mistreated American Prisoners of War, namely, Captain Ishikawa, Lt. Murada, Lt. Ando and Sergeant Moajima, were not brought to trial, as apprehension and custody of said persons had not been obtained at the time this case went to trial.

The second part of the report made a brief review of the testimony provided by the prosecution and the defence, thoroughly sorting out all the matters raised in the testimonies and arranging in logical order all that the tribunal had heard, thus demonstrating the thoroughness with which the court had assured the fairness of its proceedings. The relevant passages read as follows:

EVIDENCE:

Briefly summarized, the evidence is to the following effect:

For the Prosecution

## 1. As to GENJI MATSUDA

On 11 November 1942, 1202 American Prisoners of War arrived in Mukden (R 15), and an additional 126 arrived in December 1942 and February 1943. Colonel Genji Matsuda assumed command of his camp 2 December 1942 (R 16). The original camp known as the Mukden Prisoner of War Camp was located on the north edge of the city of Mukden, and occupied until 29 July 1943. The second camp was called the Hoten Prisoner of War Camp, and was located in the eastern section of Mukden. During the summer of 1944, three branch camps were established in the vicinity of Mukden, known as branch camps 1, 2 and 3 (R 24). The original camp consisted of from twenty to thirty wooden barracks, each being about twenty feet wide and 120 feet long, housing from sixty to ninety men (R 16, 80). Each barracks had three stoves but insufficient coal was furnished to insure adequate heat (R 80), although large quantities of coal were under the control of the Japanese Army in the city of Mukden (R 17). Sanitary conditions were poor and unclean latrines were provided (R 36).

The hospital at the first camp consisted of a wooden barracks and equipment was inadequate. Sick patients in the hospital had to get out of bed and cross frozen ground to get to the latrine. On 2 December 1942 approximately 240 internees were seriously ill in the hospital and as many as 700 attended sick call in December 1942 (R 18, 58, 59). Total deaths of American prisoners of war in December 1942 amounted to 53. In the year 1943 disease accounted for 83 deaths at the two camps under the command of Matsuda, with the death graph steadily declining from 42 in January to 1 in December (R 19). Dysentery, beri beri, pneumonia and diphtheria were the prevalent causes of death (R 25).

The food served to the prisoners of war was very scanty (R 18), and many complained of hunger during the first few months. At least thirty dogs were slaughtered and eaten by the internees (R 19, 84), as well as some snakes (R 84). A typical meal as served to the prisoners of war, which was also as served in the camp hospital was as follows: one bun, three times a day; boiled cornmeal with a little salt in the morning; for lunch a bowl of Chinese cabbage, maize, perhaps a few vegetables and later soy bean soup. The night meal was the same as for lunch (R 83).

The new camp consisted of three two-storey brick barracks, a hospital and kitchen, water plant, bath-house, assembly hall for prisoners of war and other buildings for Japanese. The enclosure around the camp was a brick wall fourteen feet high charged with electricity. There were never more than 900 prisoners of war in this camp at any one time (R 38). An inspection of the camp and hospital was made at least once each month by Matsuda (R24).

In the fall and winter of 1943 the barracks were cold until on 11 November fires were allowed. The hallways, latrine and washrooms were inadequately heated and a thick coating of ice formed over the walls and ceilings of their rooms. It was also required by the Japanese order that the floor be sprinkled with water which caused much dampness (R 39). The barracks were infested with lice and fleas from the time of the arrival of the prisoners of war until 16 April 1944 when a delousing programme was carried out (R 40).

Requests were repeatedly made to Colonel Matsuda by the staff of the American prisoner of war doctors to provide dental care for prisoners of war which were ignored.

Many of the prisoners of war went to work for the Manchurian Machine Tool Company (R 38) where machine tools were manufactured and some airplane parts were made. A protest made by the prisoners of war as to being forced to work on the airplane parts was ignored (R 39).

A report signed by approximately eighteen American officers, being (Pros. Ex. #1) states in substance that 15000 letters which had arrived as early as the latter part of 1943 were not delivered to the prisoners of war until 17 August 1945, and that most of the prisoners of war were unable to dispatch even the limited quantity of mail allowed. Canteen privileges were denied from 1 August 1943 to 17 August 1945 and that normal use of recreational equipment was denied from 27 March 1943 to 17 August 1945. Less than ten religious services were allowed to be conducted between 11 November 1942 to 29 April 1945. Many prisoners of war were confined in the guardhouse for thirty days or more without trial (R 50).

Early in 1944 replacements for worn out shoes were hard to obtain and by 5 October 1944, 135 men were entirely without shoes, except homemade sandals (R 50), however, on 5 October 1944 over 500 pairs of U.S. Army shoes were distributed, which said shoes had come through the Red Cross on or about 27 May 1944 (R 52).

No clear set of camp regulations was ever published by the Japanese for guidance of the prisoners of war, which caused many prisoners of war to be involved in infractions they knew nothing about and to be punished therefore (R 55).

On 21 June 1943 three prisoners of war escaped and were recaptured 5 July 1943. Matsuda stated the escapees would be severely punished and that the entire camp would suffer as a result of the escape. All internees in the three barracks from which the three prisoners of war escaped were required to sit at attention all day long for a period of a week to ten days (R 30).

Some of the internees were given confinement in the guardhouse from three to thirty days, and five or six internees were beaten by a lieutenant Miki, a member of the camp staff under the command of Matsuda, and then confined from 9 July 1943 to 28 October 1943. All official punishment was meted out by Matsuda, after investigation and frequent use of third degree methods by members of the latter's staff (R 31, 32). On 31 July 1943 it was officially announced the three escapees had been executed (R 32) and buried at Mukden prisoner of war cemetery (R 33), the execution having been pursuant to judgment of a military tribunal over which Matsuda had no command or control.

On 7 December 1944 the first air raid occurred at the camp. All the prisoners of war were assembled on the lower floor of their barracks and not allowed to leave the building. Prior to 7 December 1944 the Japanese personnel were provided with air raid trenches, but no protection was provided for the prisoners of war. After the first bombs had been dropped all the prisoners of war were ordered outside to lie on the parade ground. As a result of the raid, seventeen prisoners of war were killed and thirty others injured. No Japanese were killed during the raid. Prior to this raid request had been made by the prisoners of war to construct air raid shelters (R 48, 87). After this raid permission was granted for the prisoners of war to construct shelters and tools were furnished (R 56). Matsuda had never ordered the camps and hospitals to be marked to designate some as housing prisoners of war.

BEATINGS: The following Japanese personnel on Matsuda's staff beat prisoners of war:

Captain Ishikawa, second in command to Matsuda, beat approximately twenty prisoners of war (R 27).

Lt. Murada mistreated two medical officers and severely beat two enlisted men (R 27).

Lt. Ando, a superintendent officer at the camp struck two prisoners of war with his fist. On another occasion he forced the entire camp to stand at attention in the snow for approximately one hour, without overcoats, to learn the identity of a man wanted for an alleged infraction of a camp regulation (R 28). Other mistreatments by Ando (Pros. Ex. 21).

Lt. Miki, superintendent officer from 11 November 1942 to December 1943 (R 27) beat a prisoner of war with a club about three feet long about the head (R 28), and one person after such a beating was not in his right mind and died about a month later of pneumonia (R 83). Those beatings were also admitted by Miki in a statement by him (Pros. Ex. 19). Pros. Ex. 20 also refers to beatings by Miki.

Japanese Sergeant Moajima on 18 December 1944 beat to the ground prisoner of war Reardon, USN, accused of stealing a light bulb, and then Moajima ground the heel of his foot into and severely injured Reardon's face (Pros. Ex. 21).

2. As to JOICHI KUWASHIMA also known as Kawajima. He was the medical officer in charge of the hospital after 7 December 1942 (R 16, 41).

In the spring of 1943 a group of prisoners of war reported for sick call and Kuwashima or his assistant ran them around the parade ground until they fell from exhaustion (R 82). On another occasion Kuwashima diagnosed fevers of prisoners of war by feeling of their heads with his gloves on (R 90).

Every seven or eight days throughout the winter Kuwashima inspected the factory workers outside, forcing them to remove all of their clothing and shoes in extremely cold weather (R 43, 44, 84), and cases of frostbite resulted from these inspections (R 45) as well as pneumonia (Pros. Ex. 24). Other places were available indoors for these inspections (R 85). These inspections often lasted thirty to forty minutes and about 400 prisoners of war were inspected each time (Pros. Ex. 23). One prisoner of war had to have two toes amputated which were frozen from being required to stand barefooted in the snow (Pros.Ex. 30).

On 18 January 1944 at sick call, eight or ten prisoners of war fell out, three having frostbitten toes which had turned black on the ends. Kuwashima had them remove their shoes and stand barefooted on a sheet of ice with the temperature 21 degrees below zero and then stated there was no such thing as frostbite (Pros. Ex. 26).

The first Red Cross medical supplies arrived in January 1944 and the Japanese took charge of same. Before this the quantity and quality of drugs available for the internees was poor (R 40). The second shipment of Red Cross medicine arrived the latter part of May 1944 and this shipment was not unpacked until the latter part of August, and the first issue of any of this medicine occurred 19 September 1944 and was not available for prescription by prisoner of war physicians until 25 November 1944. After the medicine had been unpacked it was placed under the control of Kuwashima until he was relieved 1 November 1944 (R 41). Between 30 June 1944 and 24 November 1944 American prisoner of war doctors were denied access to the prison hospital by Kuwashima. It was also discovered that the Japanese medical corpsmen were misappropriating the Red Cross medicine during the period Kuwashima was in charge of the hospital (R 42).

After a prisoner of war, Corporal Edward S. Coley, had been confined for 31 days in the guardhouse, he had an appendicitis attack and three days later he was taken to the hospital and Kuwashima assisted in the operation. Before the operation was completed, the effect of the anesthetic wore off and no further anesthetic was allowed by Kuwashima. Whenever the prisoner groaned, Kuwashima struck him and said "No speak". After the operation Kuwashima required him to climb down from the operating table to the litter (Pros. Ex. 25).

Sufficient medicines and drugs were not allowed to be used by American prisoner of war doctors, although Red Cross medicines were available at the camp but could not be used until Kuwashima was replaced by Lt. Oki as Japanese medical officer on 25

November 1944. On 15 February 1944 prisoner of war Corporal Brister was injured in the tool factory. A small amount of serum with an expiration dated 1935 printed on the packet was furnished by Kuwashima. Corporal Brister died, but had sufficient medicine been available, Brister would probably have recovered (Pros. Ex. 28).

Prisoner of war Thomas R. Gagnet had been receiving treatment from the Japanese for his eyes until Kuwashima was placed in charge of the hospital and thereafter he was given no further medicine, although he requested such medicine from Kuwashima (R 81). Gagnet's vision is now less that 20/200 and is classified by the U.S. Army as blind (R 79).

In October 1944, prisoner of war Sergeant Thomas R. Gagnet was accused of having drunk alcohol. Kuwashima slapped him with his hand and then hit him about the head and neck with a cased saber. He was then ordered tied in a chair and a towel was tied around his mouth and nose, and water was poured in his mouth and nose. He was all wet when untied and was taken back to the guardhouse, but given no food, blankets or bedding (R 85). Some six days later Kuwashima came into the guardhouse while Gagnet was still confined and struck Gagnet with his fists about the head until Gagnet was rendered unconscious, and upon regaining consciousness discovered Kuwashima was kicking him. Gagnet's face was swollen, his eyes were black, and as late as the winter of 1945 he had nose bleeds whenever he got a cold. During his time in the guardhouse he had no food or water for the first two days and no blankets until after he had been sentenced. It was cold in the guardhouse and there was no heat at first. Gagnet's trial consisted of going before the Colonel, saluting, the charge was read, and Gagnet was sentenced by Colonel Matsuda (R 86).

Japan agreed to be bound by the Geneva Red Cross Convention and to apply mutatis mutandis to the Geneva Prisoner of War Convention (Pros. Ex. 15).

For the Defense

Gonji Matsuda stated he was responsible directly to the Commander of the Kwantung Army (R 126), that medical supplies were available from the Japanese hospital through his name, and the camp doctor made the estimates of medical supplies needed so that request for same could be made by Matsuda (R 131). He stated that Kuwashima was in charge of providing surgical care for the prisoners of war (R 132). Matsuda had requested higher medical authorities to inspect the camp to improve conditions, and some improvements were made as a result of those inspections (R 131).

Matsuda inspected part of the camp each Saturday (R 132) and he never saw any mistreatment of prisoners of war and he specifically gave orders that none should be mistreated. He also told his subordinates that the prisoners of war should be treated with all possible kindness and that they should not be kicked or struck at any time (R 133).

Matsuda never had any power or authority to appoint a court-martial for the trial of the three prisoners of war who escaped, and had no connection with the court-martial which tried them (R137).

In 1944 when the snow started to melt Matsuda announced to the prisoners that air raid shelters were going to be constructed (R 138), but after this announcement, Lt. Hiyashi reported to Matsuda that the prisoners of war did not want air raid shelters constructed as it would interfere with their baseball games by spoiling the field, which is the reason the air raid shelters were not constructed before 7 December 1944 (R 139). Later while Matsuda was in the hospital the Commander of the Kwantung Army visited the camp, and on being advised of Matsuda's plan to construct air raid shelters told Captain Ishikawa, then in charge of the camp, that there was no need to construct any air raid shelters (R 139).

After May 1945 the quantity and quality of the food served to the prisoners of war declined, but this resulted from a general food shortage and because of the fact that the Japanese were unable to purchase as formerly. The general public of Mukden were not able to procure any meat or fish for about a year and a half prior to this time (R 143). Comparable with what the general public had to go through, Matsuda claimed, the prisoners of war in the camp were much more fortunate (R 144).

Matsuda prior to his appointment as commandant of the Mukden Prisoner of War Camp had had no experience with prisoners of any kind. He received no instructions as to how to treat prisoners of war, but acted according to the regulation provided by the War Department and according to the prisoner of war dispatch regulations (R 146). Matsuda once gave Lt. Oki a small box of his personal medicine for the benefit of the prisoners of war to be used for reducing fever (R 156).

Joichi Kuwashima did not take the witness stand, but his statement was offered and received in evidence (Pros. Ex. 14).

OPINION:

It is the opinion of this office that:

a. The Military Commission was legally constituted;

b. It had jurisdiction over the persons and the offenses;

c. The evidence supports the findings of guilty; while it is true that, when contrasted with the strict rules governing court-martial cases, the procedure in war crimes cases gives wider discretion to a military commission in the admission of evidence, note is taken of the fact that the detection and proof of war crimes is made more difficult by reason of the enemy's ability to conceal or destroy the best evidence; the same rules that governed this trial and which permit the Commission to receive such evidence as "would be of assistance in proving or disproving the charges, or such as in the Commission's opinion would have probative value in the mind of a reasonable man" have been constitutionally upheld by the Supreme Court of the United States in the recent Yamashita case (66 Sup. Ct. 340);

d. The record discloses no error injuriously affecting the substantial rights of the accused; and,

e. The sentences are legal.

RECOMMENDATION:

It is accordingly recommended that the sentence be confirmed and ordered executed.

ACTION:

An action designed to carry the above recommendations into effect should they meet with your approval is submitted herewith.

On 27 January 1947, General John P Lucas, chief of the US Military Advisory Group China, signed off on this report, approving the prison term imposed on Matsuda Genji and ordering him to be held temporarily in the Huade Road prison in Shanghai pending final designation of the site of his incarceration. Matsuda was ultimately sent to Japan to serve his sentence.

On the same day, General Lucas approved the death sentence meted out to Kuwashima Joichi and ordered that it be carried out. He further ordered that Kuwashima's sentence be carried out at the Huade Road prison in Shanghai under the command of American prison authorities. Kuwashima was executed in Shanghai on 1 March 1947.

*This final chapter was part of the Research on Trials of Japanese War Criminals by the US Military Commissions in the China Theatre (16BZS078), funded by the National Social Science Fund of China.*

# AFTERWORD

The Mukden POW camp had a number of particular traits: it was highly specialised; its rate of death among the prisoners was particularly high; and it held prisoners of general officer rank. It was the result of the Japanese policy of "using war to make war". The Japanese military used prisoners of war as a resource for the making of their war of aggression, and, when their backs were to the wall, they tried to make use of their high-ranking prisoners as bargaining chips.

The establishment of their detention locale for such high-ranking POWs illustrates the intentions of the Japanese to use China's northeast, which they had controlled for years, as a 'rear area' in support of their further aggressive war and their long-term plans for the occupation of their so-called 'Manshū' – Manchuria.

The Mukden POW camp represents the tangible record of Japan's war crimes in violation of international standards and humanitarian conventions. It provides us with a basis for understanding these historical events and offers a new perspective from which to view the Pacific war itself. It enables us to see the struggle between justice and injustice in time of war, and the clash between good and evil within human nature. The brutality of the Japanese, and the suffering of the prisoners of war, unprecedented in human history and recounted in these pages, not only offer ironclad proof of wartime criminality; they also provide the human race with an urgent warning: do not forget history, cherish peace and oppose war with every fibre of your being.

History like this, in its vividness and its depth, compels us to ponder deeply the turmoil and upheavals of our own times. Inscribing history in our minds as we turn our gaze to the future, it is our responsibility to apply reason and deep reflection to our understanding of war and to work together to protect the future of humankind with all its blessings.

# BIBLIOGRAPHY

1. William J Duggan, *Silence of A Soldier*, Oakland, Elderberry Press, 2003
2. W S Ken Hughes, *Slaves of the Samurai*, Melbourne, Oxford University Press, 1946
3. Lewis A Miner, *Surrender on Cebu*, Paducah, Turner Publishing Company, 2001
4. Duane Schultz, *Hero of Bataan*, New York, St Martin's Press, 1981
5. Hal Leith, *POWs of Japanese Rescued*, Victoria, Trafford Publishing, 2003
6. Ken Towery, *The Chow Dipper*, Austin, Eakin Press, 1994
7. Oliver 'Red' Allen, *Abandoned on Bataan*, Boeren, Crimson Horse Entertainment & Publishing Company, 2002
8. Maurice A Christie, *Mission "Scapula": Special Operations in the Far East*, Stone, Panda Press (Stone) Ltd, 2004

9. Joseph A Petak, *Never Plan Tomorrow*, Fullerton, Aquataur, 1991

10. Linda Goetz Holmes, *Guests of the Emperor*, Annapolis, Naval Institute Press, 2010

11. James Bollich, *Bataan Death March: A Soldier's Story*, Gretna, Pelican Publishing Company, 2003

12. T Walter Middleton, *Flashbacks: Prisoner of War in the Philippines*, New York, Alexander Books, 2001

13. Kermit Roosevelt, *The Overseas Targets: War Report of the OSS Vol. 2*, New York, Walker Publishing Company, 1976

14. D Clayton James, *South To Bataan, North To Mukden*, Athens, University of Georgia Press, 1971

15. Brian Montgomery, *Shenton of Singapore: Governor and Prisoner of War*, London, Leo Cooper and Secker & Warburg, 1984

16. Sir John Smyth VC, *Percival and the Tragedy of Singapore*, London, Macdonald & Co., 1971

17. Richard Connaughton, *MacArthur and Defeat in the Philippines*, Woodstock & New York, The Overlook Press, 2001

18. Jonathan M Wainwright, *General Wainwright's Story*, New York, Doubleday & Company, 1946

19. Lt Gen A E Percival, *The War in Malaya*, New Delhi, Sagar Publications, 1971

20. Ronald H Spector, *In the Ruins of Empire*, New York, Random House Paperbacks, 2007

21. P Scholten, *Op Reis Met De 'Special Party'*, Leiden, A.W. Sijthoff Leiden, 1971

22. John M Beebe, *Prisoner of the Rising Sun*, College Station, Texas A&M University Press, 2006

23. Roger Hilsman, *American Guerrilla: My War Behind Japanese Lines*, Washington D.C., Potomac Books, 2005

24. John K Singlaub, *Hazardous Duty*, New York, Summit Books, 1991

25. Andrew Faulkner, *Arthur Blackburn, VC*, South Australia, Wakefield Press, 2008

26. Oliver Lindsay, *The Battle of Hong Kong*, Gloucestershire, Spellmount, 2005

27. William C Braly, *The Hard Way Home*, Washington D.C., Washington Infantry Journal Press, 1947

28. Clifford Kinvig, *Scapegoat: General Percival of Singapore*, London, Brassey's, 1996

29. Sheldon Zimbler, *Undaunted Valor: The Men of Mukden*, Kingston, NY, Tri-State Publishing, 2008

30. Marcel Junod, *Warrior Without Weapons*, International Committee of the Red Cross, 1982

31. Trial Transcript, the War Crimes Trial of Genji Matsuda, Volume II, Folder 5, Box 1660, Entry 1321, RG 331, NARA（美国国家档案馆）。

32. 《A级極東国際軍事裁判記録（英文）》，JACAR：Ref.A08071261100，（日）国立公文書館。

33. 《俘虜情報局ノ業務ニ就テ》，JACAR：Ref.A14110158800,俘情局，（日）国立公文書館。

34. 《陸軍北方部隊略歴之関東直轄部隊》，JACAR：Ref.C12122425200，厚生省救援局，（日）防衛省防衛研究所。

35. 《俘虜に関する諸法規類集》，JACAR: Ref. C13070713200，（日）防省防研究所。

36. 茶园义男，《BC级战犯米军上海等裁判资料》，东京：不二出版，1989年。

37. 茶园义男，《BC级战犯中国·仏国裁判资料》，东京：不二出版，1992年。

38. 茶園義男，《大東亜戦争下外地俘虜収容所》，东京：不二出版，1996年。

39. 茶園義男，《滿洲移民拓務局原資料》，东京：不二出版社，1990年。

40. 新田満夫，《極東國際軍事審判速記錄》（第1–10卷），东京：雄松堂书店，1968年。

41. 林博史，《BC 級戰犯裁判》，东京：岩波新书株式会社，2005年。

42. 内海爱子，《日本军の俘虜政策》，东京：青木书店，2005年。

43. 西里扶甬子，《生物戰部隊 731》，东京：草の根出版社，2002年。

44. 秦郁彦，《日本陸海軍總合事典》，东京：东京大学出版会，2005年。

45. 桑岛治三郎，《殉国の軍医大尉》，东京：日本医事新报社，1993年。

46. 朱贵生、王振德、张椿年等，《第二次世界大战史》，人民出版社，2005年。

47. 罗兹·墨著、黄磷译，《亚洲史》，商务印书馆，2005年。

48. R.R. 帕尔默等著，《近现代世界史》（下册），北京大学出版社，2009年。

49. 袁间琨：《沈阳历史大事本末》（下卷），辽宁人民出版社，2002年。

50. 步平、荣维木主编，《中华民族抗日战争全史》，中国青年出版社，2010年。

# ACKNOWLEDGMENTS

I first came across the topic of the Mukden POW camp by chance during the course of my work. It has now been more than 20 years since I threw myself into researching it. Looking back on the journey of this research, although there have been repeated obstacles, I never lost the drive to keep pushing forwards.

The biggest challenge I encountered was the lack of historical documents. Much of the original Japanese documentation was destroyed or incompletely decoded, so there were limits to how much and where I could obtain the information. Relevant documents were also stored in several other countries including the US, the UK, the Netherlands, Australia and New Zealand, which increased the difficulty of collecting and using them. Within China, there were only a few isolated historical documents. Although best efforts have been made to collect the evidence in the archives and libraries of these countries, there remains a lack of complete and systematic historical documentation.

Therefore, the most practical research route has been the inclusion of face-to-face interviews with the former POWs and their descendants, as well as Chinese labourers and Japanese veterans.

Audio documentation has been created from these interviews and then cross-referenced with the paper evidence. My research has always been based on the historical facts, and my aim has always been to paint a full portrait of life in the Mukden POW camp.

If there are any errors in this book, I welcome criticism or corrections from readers. For this English-language edition, source materials in multiple languages that were rendered into Chinese have now been translated into English. This has been a challenging process, and although every effort has been made to preserve the words of the original texts, the language barriers might have resulted in some loss of meaning.

During the process, I was fortunate to discover little-known historical events. Meeting the surviving POWs was a rare opportunity to converse with history. Through the interviews, I established new friendships with those veterans. They expressed their concerns and care for my country, where they suffered such hardships, and they now regard China as their spiritual home. One of the interviewees, Walt Huss, an American POW, saw a picture of Shenyang people celebrating Spring Festival in his local newspaper; he cut the picture out and posted it to me. One summer, there were floods in the area surrounding Shenyang, and he worriedly asked about the situation. Shenyang has become a place that the surviving POWs care about, and that gives me the incentive to keep going with the research.

Working on this book has been an emotional experience for me. I want to thank the POW survivors who supported my research for all these years. I want to mention one of the interviewees in particular: the American veteran Oliver Allen, who passed away on 15 July 2015 while the original Chinese version of this book was being published. Many years ago, he told me to be prepared to lose some of the friends I would make during my research. This is a fact of life. I am saddened by the deaths of the veterans I have met over the years. I also feel the urgency of accelerating the research. I wish I could do better.

My thanks also go to the fellow researchers who provided assistance and references for this book.

Finally, from the bottom of my heart, I would like to thank the People's Publishing House who invited me to publish this book and help the little-known history of the Mukden POW camp to become better understood by the public.

Yang Jing
November 2018

*The author visits Oliver Allen (Mukden POW #362) in*
*Taylor, Texas, 6 May 2007*